wedding floristry

wedding floristry

LYNDA OWEN

Hodder & Stoughton

A MEMBER OF THE HODDER HEADLINE GROUP

A catalogue record for this title is available from the British Library

ISBN 0 340 60485 9

First published 1994
Impression number   10 9 8 7 6 5 4 3 2 1
Year   1998 1997 1996 1995 1994

Typeset by Wearset, Boldon, Tyne and Wear.
Printed in Hong Kong for Hodder & Stoughton Educational, a division of
Hodder Headline Plc, 338 Euston Road, London NW1 3BH by
Colorcraft Ltd.

With love and thanks to my mother, Joan Saunders –
my mentor, friend and inspiration.

*A*cknowledgements

For their friendly service and supplying all the flowers for the photography, my thanks go to a great bunch of guys at:

Geest Wholesale Services
Staniers Way
Hereford HR1 1JU

I would also like to thank the following:

Martyn and Gina
Hair Stylists
Inspiration
College Street
Worcester

Diane Clark Wedding Cakes
3 May Tree Hill
Droitwich Spa
Worcestershire

Robin Sandry
Artistic Photographer
The Studio
Tannery Mews
Carden Street
Worcester

Fownes Resort Hotel
City Walls Road
Worcester

My special thanks go to my partner, Joan Saunders, and the staff of Floral Roundabout, Worcester, for their continued support, especially Annette Moule.

The author and publisher would also like to thank Eileen Nott for supplying the flowers and floristry tools featured on the cover, and Kate Simunek for providing the beautiful illustrations.

Contents

Preface

For the professional florist, a wedding is a chance to help dreams come true for a day. In no other area of floristry do you need greater expertise to guide, to advise and to create designs of timeless beauty for that special day.

This book gives an insight into wedding floristry, showing the fundamental techniques and qualities of good workmanship that are basic to all bridal designs. This is the foundation on which to build, one step leading naturally to the next, developing professional selling skills and creativity as your knowledge grows.

Wedding floristry is constantly changing to encompass the prevailing fashions. Further study should include the history of bridal fashion to enable you to design a bouquet for any style of dress.

While giving broad, practical guidelines on making bridal bouquets, the emphasis in this book is on exercising the imagination to stimulate creativity. Making choices for yourself and learning from your own experiments and observations is the best teaching method of all. The principles and elements of design will help build your design knowledge, but they are not restrictions and should never impede your natural flair and originality.

Transforming a group of flowers into a design where each individual becomes part of a whole concept – your unique creation – should be the aim of every professional florist.

Above all, I hope my enthusiasm will shine through – inspiring you to create designs which every bride will cherish.

Introduction

For the bride and her entourage, coming to the florist to discuss the wedding flowers is a very important occasion. It may be just another wedding to the florist, but to the bride it is one of the most important days of her life. Realising this and giving the bride your full and special attention will result in a sale.

Generally, brides are unsure of the flowers and style of bouquet they should choose. They come to the florist for help and advice. A friendly, confident approach is necessary to reassure the bride that you are a professional, capable of taking the order and executing it perfectly. The order will be lost if the florist simply produces a book of wedding designs and expects the bride to choose from this without any assistance. The florist cannot deal adequately with a bridal order while also trying to serve bunches of flowers or answer the telephone. The wedding order needs individual attention. Far better to make an appointment for the bride when you can give her your undivided attention. **An evening appointment can be worthwhile.**

The bride's mother will often have plenty of ideas of what her daughter should carry, and she may get carried away in her enthusiasm. Remember that, for the bride's mother, this is an anxious time – she wants her daughter's wedding to be perfect. By taking command in a relaxed, friendly manner, the florist will reassure her that the order is in the right hands.

On the first visit the bride should pay a deposit to secure the wedding date in the florist's diary. An appointment is then made approximately two months before the wedding to discuss all the details. By this time the bride will have purchased the wedding dresses and swatches of material will be available. Most florist shops keep a wedding diary. Check in this first to ensure the date is available before taking the order. Many florist shops do not take weddings at peak periods, or have a policy of taking only a limited number of weddings per week. Overbooking will result in complaints.

Taking a wedding order

Only a senior florist should take a wedding order. To help the bride choose the best designs takes a wealth of background knowledge which only comes from several years' experience.

When the bride arrives for her consultation, a quiet area should have been reserved – preferably with seating – so that discussions can be made privately and in comfort.

See Plate 1 on page 12

Choosing the designs

The bride will want to know how the finished bouquet will look, and the florist will want to show her examples and pictures of bouquets that would be suitable. Having a few samples of silk flower wedding bouquets and headdresses, made up in various styles, can therefore be an advantage. The bride can handle these and they can provide a good indication of what size the bouquet and headdress should be. A book of designs should also be at hand. Ideally these should show the florist's own work. If this is not possible, there are books available to purchase or the florist can make his or her own. This must look professional (a wedding photograph album could be used) and the pictures should be changed periodically to reflect the latest styles.

From the bride, the florist will want:

- swatches of dress material for the bride and bridesmaids;
- pictures or sketches of the dresses;
- any special requests for particular flowers or styles of bouquet;
- preferences for colour, or special themes.

Choosing the flowers

Although most flowers can be bought throughout the year, seasonal variations do occur. Remembering this when advising the bride will help to avoid any disappointments. Impossible requests from the bride must be dealt with firmly. It is no good taking an order that stands little chance of being fulfilled. If the bride has requested a particular flower that is definitely out of season, then it is up to the florist to offer alternative flowers of similar appearance or colour.

Trends and fashions in bridal wear mean that wedding dresses can change dramatically from season to season. The bride has a very wide range to choose from. Keeping up to date with current fashions is an integral part of a florist's knowledge, together with information on the history of bridal fashion. Generally fashions revolve, and styles from yesteryear reappear quite regularly.

Wedding Order Form

Date of wedding .... Day .... Time ....

Bride's name and address ....

....

Telephone number ....

Bride's bouquet ....

    Colour ....

    Style ....

Flower varieties ....

Brief description of dress ....

....

Cost   £

Bride's headdress ....

Cost   £

Bridesmaids' bouquets .... Number of bridesmaids ....

    Colour ....

    Style ....

Flower varieties ....

Brief description of dresses ....

....

Age of bridesmaids .... Cost   £

Bridesmaids' headdresses ....

.... Cost   £

Bride and groom's mothers' corsages ....

Style and colour of dresses ....

Flower varieties .... Cost   £

Guests' corsages ....

....

....

.... Cost £

Buttonholes ....

....

Groom's buttonhole .... Cost £

Church flowers Name of church ....

Keys kept at ....

....

....

.... Cost £

Reception flowers

Name and address of venue ....

....

....

.... Cost £

Thank you gifts ....

Delivery address ....

Total cost	£	
Delivery	£	
VAT	£	
Total	£	
Less deposit	£	
Grand total	£	

Payment is required one week prior to wedding.

Signature of bride ....

1

The bride's personality may give the florist a clue to the type of bouquet which would suit her best. Physical attributes such as height, hair colour and complexion also play an important part when choosing the perfect design. **The aim is to guide the bride into choosing flowers that will complement and enhance her overall appearance on the wedding day.**

Additional sales

Nothing looks lovelier than a fresh flower headdress exactly matching the bouquet, or a special buttonhole for the bridegroom made of flowers co-ordinating with the bride's bouquet. As you are discussing the bouquets, the opportunity to sell headdresses, buttonholes, reception and church flowers, cake decorations, thank you bouquets, and other items will arise. **Make sure you grasp these opportunities to create additional sales.**

The more the bride orders, the greater the chance of creating a stunning wedding. You will then have the opportunity to create a unique theme running throughout the entire day, using your special design skills to make the flowers memorable.

The florist must convey enthusiasm to the bride and provide an expert and efficient service. Don't forget that there will be many unmarried friends of the bride at the wedding – all potential customers.

Completing the order form

Armed with all this information, the wedding order can now be taken. It is important that every detail is recorded on paper. A special wedding order form (see page 2) should be used, with space for every relevant detail. You may not be the person who makes up the order, so the workroom will need the fullest details to enable them to fulfil the order correctly.

The day, date and time of the wedding, together with delivery addresses and instructions, are the most important details. A brief description of the dresses should be written on the order form, including the colour and texture of material if no samples are available. (This also applies to the outfits of the bride and groom's mothers.)

Make a note of any special preferences or particular dislikes. Some brides can be superstitious and this should be recorded. If the bridesmaids are children, the ages should be noted so that the bouquets can be made to a suitable size.

Cultivar and variety names

A sound knowledge of flowers and their variety names is essential in filling out an order form. Common names such as love-in-a-mist, grape hyacinths and madonna lilies are charming and will conjure up romantic pictures in the mind for the bride. Common names, however, are regional. The wholesalers in other parts of the country or Holland, for example, might not know these names. Latin names are used universally by florists, wholesalers and horticulturists. They are therefore an important part of a professional florist's knowledge.

Consider writing on a wedding order, 'a posy of pink roses', without adding the variety name. Two months have passed since the order was made – a number of other brides have been seen and many other orders taken. There are so many shades of pink; will you be able to remember the correct shade required? A terrible mistake could occur. This is why cultivar and variety names are so important.

Cost

The cost of the bouquets will be a major factor in clinching the order. It is wise to find out if there is a fixed budget. This will determine what bouquets to suggest. A range of different priced bouquets should be offered to all brides so that no order is turned away – from a reasonably priced economy range to a designer range where bouquets are exclusively created and money is not an important aspect.

Throughout the order-taking procedure, the bride should be advised of the cost of the individual items. Once the order has been completed, the florist should then total up the amounts in front of the bride, adding VAT and delivery charges where necessary. On leaving the shop, the bride should be fully aware how much the total cost will be. Once this has been agreed, the bride should sign the order and take a duplicate copy. In this way no misunderstanding can occur over costs.

Final check

Generally, the bride will contact the florist the week before the wedding to order additional buttonholes. This is an ideal opportunity for the florist to go over the whole order with the bride, to check that all the details are correct and that nothing has been altered. **If necessary, telephone the bride a few days prior to the day to check the details. If nothing else, it reassures her of your interest.**

The florist's working tools

Trained professional craftsmen and women, in whatever field, can be recognised by the way they care for the tools of their trade. All professional trades rely on the right equipment to do the job successfully. The florist's tools are vital – without them no floristry can be accomplished.

Ideally, each florist should have his or her own tools in the workroom. It is a good idea to keep these in a small bag, pouch or pencil case, clearly marked with your name.

There are five essential floristry tools:

- Knife
- Floristry scissors
- Secateurs
- Wire cutters
- Ribbon scissors

The knife, without doubt, is the most important. A small sturdy knife with a short blade is particularly suitable. Use a knife when cutting most stems – it is far quicker than using scissors and makes a sharper, more precise cut. (*See Fig. 2.1.*)

When purchasing floristry scissors, always buy a good quality pair and try them in the hand first for comfort. Never cut wires with floristry scissors as this will make them blunt and may damage them. A pair of wire cutters will make a much neater cut.

Secateurs are needed to cut strong, woody stems and branches that would prove difficult for a knife or floristry scissors. These will be essential for church decoration, when the stems of flowers and foliage may be much thicker than those used in bridal bouquets.

Ribbon cannot be cut with floristry scissors as these will tear the fabric. A small pair of sewing scissors is therefore useful for cutting ribbons, braids and fabrics.

See Plate 2 on page 13

Floristry scissors
Ribbon scissors
Secateurs
Florist's short blade knife
Long blade knife (for foam cutting)
Pot tape in various widths, green and white
Tape (gutta-percha), green and white
Tying rafia or string
Corsage pins
German pins
Glue gun and glue sticks
Stapler and staples
Paper towel or tissues
Tissue paper
Polythene sheeting
Reel wires, various gauges
Selection of wires of differing gauges and lengths
Water spray
Waterproof plasters

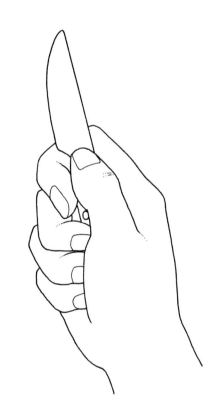

Fig. 2.1   The correct way to hold the florist's knife

Good workmanship

For the professional florist, there is no substitute for good workmanship. No matter how great the skill in design, the highest degree of technical knowledge and expertise is also required. Meticulous attention to detail, neat work and careful assembly techniques divide the specialist from the amateur. Nowhere is this more important than in wedding floristry, where bridal bouquets and accessories are seen at very close quarters. All work should be light in weight, easy to carry or wear, a joy to look at and a pleasure to hold. This high standard of fundamental technique will initially demand constant practice, but the reward will be truly proficient floristry.

Good workmanship starts at the work bench. Always have a clean, dry work area. All the materials needed to make the particular piece of floristry should be at hand. To one side of the table should be all the dry items:

- Wire containers
- Cloth or kitchen towel
- Tapes and reel wires
- Ribbon
- Adhesive tape (if necessary)
- Scissors and knife
- Glue gun

On the opposite side of the bench should be the flowers and foliage needed, in water. A water sprayer will also be required.

Keep electrical appliances well away from water.

Wired flowers can be placed on tissue paper or, alternatively, a pot with dry foam will hold the flowers on their wire stems and protect them from damage until ready for assembly. Invest in a good bouquet holder – an invaluable piece of equipment. Never lay a bouquet down on the bench as this will damage the flowers and ruin the design. Spray the flowers with water regularly and cover with polythene until ready to use.

Keeping the work area tidy and working methodically will become habits which will save time and energy. Work tools become misplaced easily in a cluttered environment.

Wires and wiring techniques

Wires are used for a variety of reasons in wedding floristry; to support the stem or flower head, to provide secure anchorage into a base, and to enable the florist to control and manipulate the flower and stem without breakage.

Selecting the right gauge of wire for the many different flowers can be confusing and, in the beginning, help will be needed to choose the correct wire. Recognising the various wires and understanding wiring techniques is important. Wires come in a range of lengths and thicknesses; handling them and practising wiring in the workroom is the first step towards achieving the fine balance between under- and over-wiring. Labelling all the wire holders in the workroom with the correct wire gauge will be a great help when selecting a wire.

Flowers should not be wired with such rigidity that they become stiff and unnatural. The wire should be just heavy enough to support the flower, yet light enough to maintain its natural movement. A slightly tremulous effect is desirable. **Emphasis must be given to the natural movement of the flowers.**

Support wiring

It is not necessary to support wire all flower stems in a bridal bouquet – only those in vulnerable positions (such as the extremity or outline of a design), focal flowers, flowers with weak stems, and any that could become damaged while the bouquet is being carried. Over-wiring will result in a bouquet which is heavy, rigid and difficult to carry. Under-wiring could mean the bouquet will lose its shape. (*See Fig. 3.1.*)

Mount wiring

Sometimes it is necessary to add a wire to the base of a stem, to add extra security when fixing and to provide a firm anchorage. This method is used when the mount wires form part of the handle in a wired bouquet and for added security when fixing stems into foam holders. Generally, a stronger wire is required for this. There are two methods of mount wiring; double-leg mounting (*Fig. 3.2*) and single-leg mounting (*Fig. 3.3*).

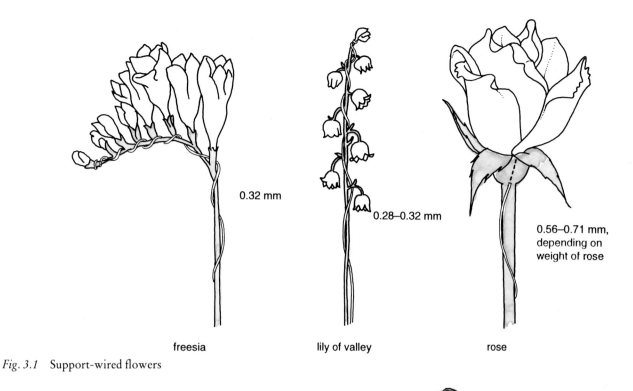

0.32 mm

0.28–0.32 mm

0.56–0.71 mm, depending on weight of rose

freesia

lily of valley

rose

Fig. 3.1   Support-wired flowers

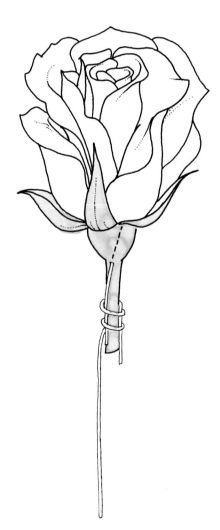

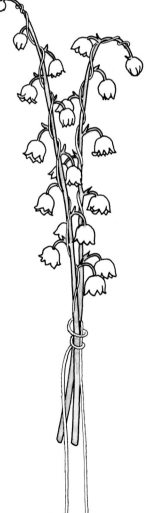

Fig. 3.2   Single-leg mount

Fig. 3.3   Double-leg mount

Control

Wiring is also used to control flowers and foliage so that they may be more easily manipulated in a design. Only the finest wires are used.

Wiring flowers is a necessity in bridal floristry, but restraint must be used. The natural form and shape of the flower and its stem can be destroyed by over-wiring. **Rigid wiring has no place in modern floristry.**

Guide to wire use

Wire Gauge Chart

GAUGE	Metric	Old
	1.25 mm	18 swg
	1.00 mm	19 swg
	0.90 mm	20 swg
	0.71 mm	22 swg
	0.56 mm	24 swg
	0.46 mm	26 swg
	0.38 mm	28 swg
	0.32 mm	30 swg
	0.28 mm	32 swg
	0.24 mm	34 swg
	0.20 mm	36 swg
LENGTH	Metric	Old
	90 mm	3½"
	130 mm	5"
	180 mm	7"
	230 mm	9"
	260 mm	10"
	310 mm	12"
	360 mm	14"
	460 mm	18"

Stub wires are sold by weight, in bundles of one gauge and length. The weight per bundle is 2½ kg (6 lb). They can be bought covered with a green plastic coating, which is ideal for support wiring. Thinner wires can be obtained, coated in silver or green. Reel wires are useful for binding and for some fine support wiring. Again, these can be bought with a variety of finishes.

In wedding floristry, generally only the finest wires are used. The following list gives the most popular wires used for bridal work. This is intended only as a guideline – the florist will have to decide when viewing the flower, its weight, length and stem thickness, which is the best wire to use.

0.71 mm (22 swg)	Used as a support wire for large roses, carnations and similar flowers. Used as a mount wire in bridal bouquets.
0.56 mm (24 swg)	Used extensively for wedding floristry as a support and mount wire.
0.38 mm (28 swg)	Used for wiring florets and larger leaves. Some mounting for lightweight flowers.
0.32 mm (30 swg)	Used for wiring small florets and small leaves (e.g. *Hedera helix*).
0.24 mm (34 swg)	Used as a reel wire for binding, and for supporting very fine, delicate flowers.

There are many floristry terms for the wiring procedures used. Some of them are explained below.

Stitching

Stitching is a type of support wiring, generally used for leaves. Always use a silver- or green-coated wire, as uncovered wires could cause damage. There are two methods of stitching. The most widely used method is to make small stitches three-quarters of the way up the main vein (*Fig. 3.4*). For larger leaves, small stitches are threaded up the main vein and closed neatly at the tip (*Fig. 3.5*).

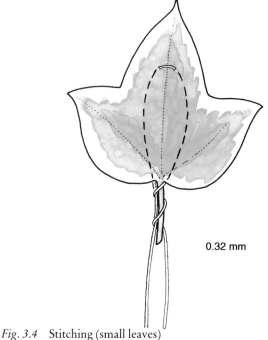

0.32 mm

Fig. 3.4 Stitching (small leaves)

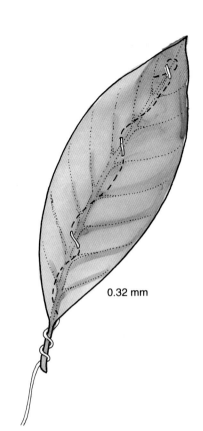

Feathering

In feathering, several petals are taken from a whole flower (e.g. a carnation) then wired together to form a small flower (*Fig. 3.7*). Feathering is a very time consuming procedure.

0.32 mm

Fig. 3.5   Stitching (large leaves)

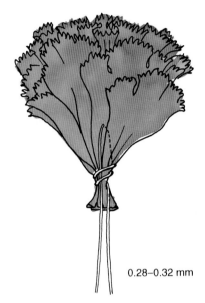

0.28–0.32 mm

Pipping

Pipping is the term used when single florets are taken from a flower (e.g. hyacinth pips) and wired individually (*Fig. 3.6*).

Fig. 3.7   Feathering

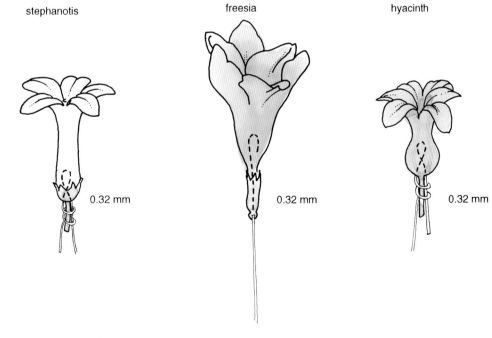

stephanotis

freesia

hyacinth

0.32 mm

0.32 mm

0.32 mm

Fig. 3.6   Pipping

Units

When a number of flowers are joined together on one wire, this is called a unit. The function of a unit is to reduce the number of wires going through the binding point in a bouquet. This is essential in a large wedding bouquet, where too many wires will make it heavy to carry. There are several types of units.

Fig. 3.8   Branching unit

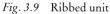

Fig. 3.9   Ribbed unit

Branching unit

The branching unit is a group of materials, usually of one colour and type, fashioned to look as natural as possible – almost as though they grew that way. Generally the smallest flower is used at the tip, working down to the largest at the base (*Fig. 3.8*).

Ribbed unit

The ribbed unit can be made either of materials of the same type and colour or of a mixture of colours and materials. No stem is seen between each flower. This type of unit is useful for making garlands and circlets (*Fig. 3.9*).

Natural unit

The natural unit consists of flowers and foliage on their own stems, arranged to look as natural and uncontrived as possible. The stems are support wired only when necessary and a mount wire is used for anchorage (*Fig. 3.10*).

Fig. 3.10   Natural unit

Taping

Once the flowers have been wired, the wires must be concealed with a protective covering (*Fig. 3.11*). Over the years, florists have covered wires with a variety of materials. Thin strips of crêpe paper and silver paper were wrapped around the wire before tapes became commercially available. Without any covering, the wires will look unsightly and may rust. This could cause damage to an expensive gown.

Tapes, sometimes called gutta-percha, are water repellent and can be bought in a variety of colours. The most popular are shades of green and brown. When the wires are taped with these, they take on the appearance of a natural stem or branch. White tape has a very limited use as it can look stark and unnatural.

Tapes can be damaged by excessive cold or heat, so keep them in a frost-free position away from direct heat. There are many makes of tape available – choose one which has some elasticity and will stretch to give a thin, neat covering to the wire.

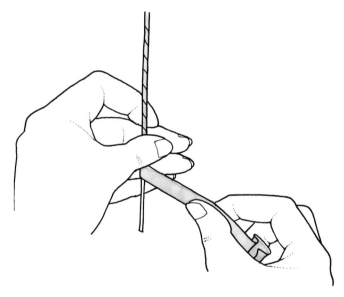

Fig. 3.11   Taping

Using glue

Although traditional wiring and anchorage methods will always be used, there are alternative fixing processes at the florist's disposal. Glue is used extensively in wedding floristry for securing flowers, ribbons and other materials into designs.

There are two types of glue gun available. The hot-glue gun emits a very hot, liquid glue. This will stick items immediately, but care must be taken as the hot glue can burn the skin. In the low-heat glue gun, the glue has been cooled before it is ejected. The cool glue will therefore not damage or burn delicate, fresh flowers or fine materials. Both types of gun have their uses.

Glue dips can also be very useful as several people can use them at once, eliminating a queue for the glue gun. The glue melts into a pot or tray, and the stem is then dipped into the glue and secured into position.

When using glue, use only sufficient amount to stick the item securely. Too much glue can be unsightly, leaving cobwebs and fine trails over the design.

Headdresses can be made very quickly when using the glueing method. Remember, the same principles of good workmanship apply whatever method of construction is used.

Great care must always be taken when using electrical appliances.

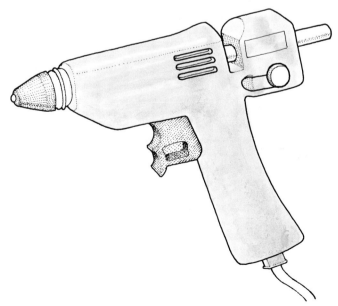

Plate 1 Discussing the wedding order

Plate 2 Floristry tools

Plate 3 Autumn flowers and foliage

Colour

Of all the tools at a florist's disposal, colour is the most powerful. It can evoke a mood, capture a personality and inspire a theme. It can suggest mystery, be subtle and gentle, or fiery and passionate. Colour is of greater importance than any other design element when choosing flowers for a wedding. Choosing creative colour schemes is an art in itself and, as florists, we have to learn how to select the best colour schemes for the occasion. Some people are born with an intuitive sense of colour – the ability to create imaginative colour schemes easily and naturally. For others colour is something that has to be learnt. Dealing with flowers every day in many shades and hues gives the florist the opportunity to experiment and to discover which colours blend best with others.

The colour wheel

The colour wheel (*Fig. 4.1 on page 16*) helps explain how colours react and relate to one another. When in doubt, the colour wheel can be of invaluable help when trying to get the best harmony.

Primary colours
Red, blue, yellow – these form the basis of all other colours. Primary colours cannot be created by mixing colours (*Fig. 4.2 on page 16*).

Secondary colours
Orange, green, violet – these are colours which can be obtained by mixing equal amounts of two primary colours (*Fig. 4.3 on page 17*).

Colour harmonies

There are many recognised colour harmonies – colours that complement, contrast or blend smoothly with one another. These can be a tremendous guide when experimenting with colour.

Monochromatic
A monochromatic colour scheme uses tints, tones and shades of one colour (*Fig. 4.4 on page 17*). It is easy to accomplish a pleasing result using this popular colour harmony. It can be bland, however, if differing depths of colour are not used.

Analagous
Analagous colours lie next to each other on the colour wheel (*Fig. 4.9 on page 20*). An analagous colour harmony can comprise two, three or four colours, generally with only one primary colour. These schemes have variety and interest.

Complementary
Complementary colours lie exactly opposite on the colour wheel – they contrast most strongly with one another (*Fig. 4.10 on page 20*). This can be a vibrant, exciting harmony as the colours will intensify each other. However, using both colours at equal strength can be very tiring to the eye.

Triadic
The triadic colour scheme is made up of three colours equidistant on the colour wheel (*Fig. 4.11 on page 21*). Generally, one colour is dominant and the second and third are used in smaller quantities. If equal amounts of all three colours are used, it can produce an undesirable static look.

Other colour schemes which can be used with brilliant success, if the florist is a skilled colourist, are tetriadic and polychromatic colour harmonies.

Tetriadic
A tetriadic colour scheme uses four colours at equal distance from each other on the colour wheel (*Fig. 4.12 on page 21*). As with a triadic colour harmony, different degrees of each colour should be used.

Polychromatic
A polychromatic scheme makes indiscriminate use of many colours (also called psychedelic when using colours of pure hue). Mixed colours can present a pretty garden effect if pastel shades are used.

Choosing flower colours

Colours in flowers vary enormously and can also change dramatically as the flowers mature and open. This is worthwhile remembering, as the flowers should look good throughout the wedding day. In bridal work, it is vitally important that the florist considers the background colour of the dresses, as this will affect the colours chosen for the bouquets. Colours react differently when placed in front of others. The florist must visualise the effect of the bouquet against the dress.

Like all fashion, colour trends vary with the seasons. The florist's job is to produce colour harmonies that will give pleasure to the bride. She will have spent considerable time choosing her colour scheme and the whole look could be ruined by the wrong choice of flower colours. It is easy to be unimaginative and safe, with boring colour schemes such as pink and white or yellow and white. These schemes are safe because most brides will accept them, not knowing that more interesting harmonies could be achieved. They have no place for the skilled colourist.

Think about the season in which the wedding is taking place. An autumn wedding can be a magical mixture of earth colours, teamed with the colour of ripening corn and the rich gold/orange of autumnal leaves. Together with berries or hops, this is the work of an inspired florist (**see Plate 3**). In the winter, when days are dark, the florist might have to choose colours which are brighter and more easily visible. Colours most visible in poor light are yellow, yellow/orange, and yellow/green. They have greater luminosity than other colours, which will be particularly important when decorating dark churches. Colours can appear warm or cool. Fiery reds, hot pinks, and burnished golds can look wonderful on a cold winter day. Similarly, ice blues and tranquil greens can bring freshness to a hot summer day.

The colours chosen by the bride will probably reflect her personality. Pastel shades have always been popular for wedding gowns – soft and gentle, they conjure up the ideal picture of an English wedding. The more adventurous bride may choose more luxuriant, vibrant colours.

Colour is the most powerful medium for the florist to capture the imagination of the bride.

Take a fresh look at colours around you. Observe, experiment and, most of all, study nature for the finest examples of exquisite colourings.

Principles of design

The principles of design provide a florist with guidelines. How these are then used will determine the merits of the finished design.

Sometimes design ideas are difficult to develop. To be truly creative, the florist will need to plan and organise and have a clear mental picture of how the finished design will look. **A master plan or mental blue print is essential to accomplish any good piece of floristry.**

Knowledge of the design principles will be an invaluable asset when discovering your own style and developing your creativity. Often it will be necessary to fall back on these basic principles when trying something new, or to aid constructive thinking. The principles of design should never restrict or inhibit – they are there to guide and help, not to overpower. The adventurous florist will want to challenge and stretch these principles, to produce work of flair and imagination.

Some of the major principles of design are:

- Proportion/scale
- Balance
- Rhythm
- Harmony
- Repetition
- Dominance

The most important elements of design are:

- Colour
- Form
- Space
- Texture

General guidelines for interesting designs

1 Vary the stem lengths within the design, recessing some flowers low into the bouquet to give depth to the design.

2 Study the way flowers grow. Use them to their greatest effect, naturally, not all facing forwards. Make use of curved stems and trailing foliage. Look for the flower's direction of growth and use it in this natural way.

3 Have some areas of dominance in the design. Focal areas can be created by using round shapes, brighter colours, and shiny or heavy textured materials.

4 Do not clutter a design with too many flowers or foliage. Space can be a hidden asset. Learn to value space and work with it as a design element (*Fig. 4.5*).

5 Group flowers of similar shape or colour together, creating patterns within the bouquet. This will give unity and rhythm to any design.

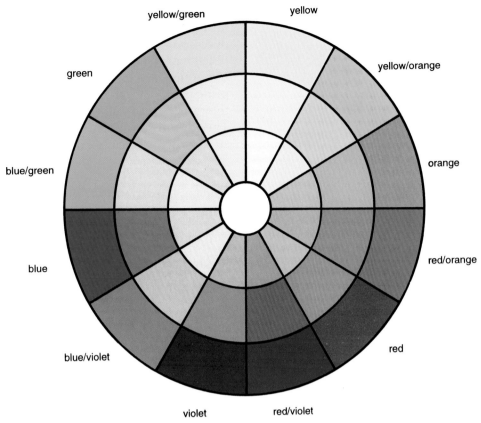

Fig. 4.1 Colour wheel showing pure hue with addition of white

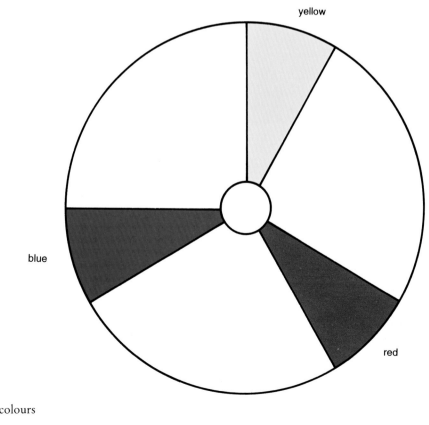

Fig. 4.2 Primary colours

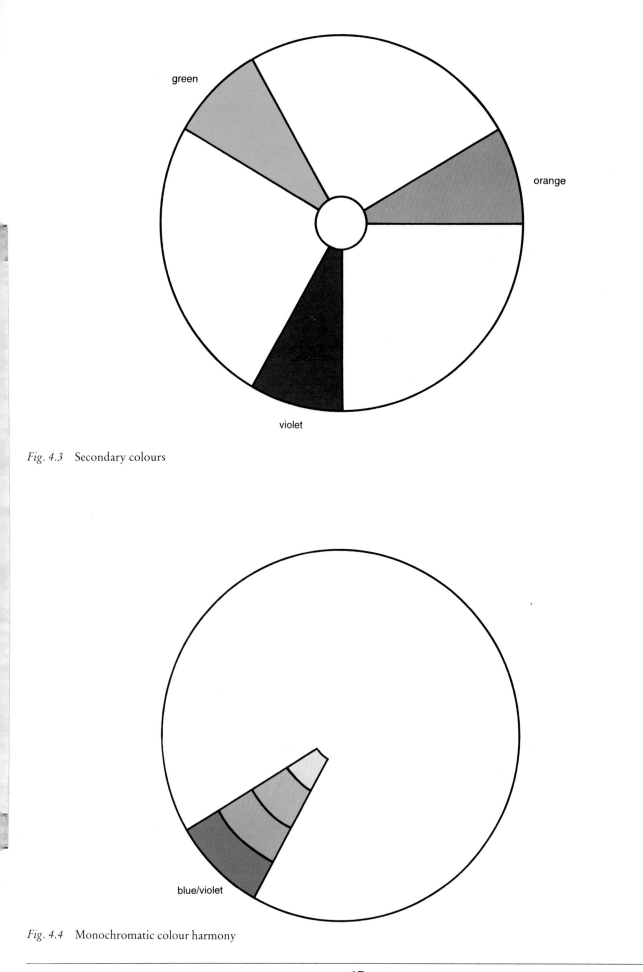

Fig. 4.3   Secondary colours

Fig. 4.4   Monochromatic colour harmony

4

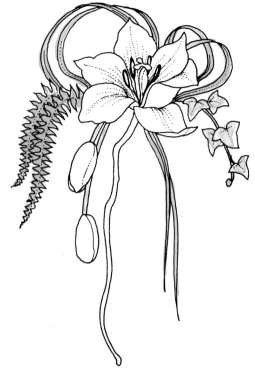

Fig. 4.5 Using space within the design can be a hidden asset

6 Use a contrast of shapes and textures to add interest to the design. Arrangements using flowers of only one shape and size can be boring and static (*Fig. 4.6*).

Fig. 4.6 Use a variety of shapes and textures

7 The size and proportions of the bouquet will be determined by the height and size of the bride and the style of dress worn. Remember, a bride looks taller in a long dress with a cathedral train. In this case, a longer bouquet could be more appropriate.

8 Simplicity can be the key to the most creative bridal bouquets. Try not to complicate or confuse. Break the design down into the fewest shapes and lines as possible. Simplicity can often be the most successful principle of all (*Fig. 4.7*).

Fig. 4.7 Simplicity can often be the most successful design principle

9 When designing the bouquets, the location of the wedding should be considered (e.g. registry office, cathedral, village church) to achieve the correct sense of occasion.

10 Use the visual weight of the flowers to create an interesting balance within the design. Even in a symmetrical design, placement of materials does not have to be identical to achieve visual balance. Using a group of small flowers to balance a large bloom can be more exciting to look at than using flowers of equal size.

Choosing the best flowers

The beauty of the bridal bouquet will need to last for many hours. Throughout the marriage ceremony and on into the reception, guests will be looking at the flowers. One of the most important tasks, therefore, is choosing flowers and foliage that will have long lasting qualities. It is here that a florist's knowledge and expertise comes to the fore. The professional florist should know which flowers to avoid and which blooms will stay turgid and fresh longest. Immature foliage will wilt rapidly and must be avoided.

Careful thought about the colour and varieties of flowers to be used is important. Flowers will be chosen for their colour, shape and perfume. Foliage is an essential element within the design, which will enhance and complement the flowers. There is a good variety of commercially grown foliage available. Do not dismiss garden foliage which, if conditioned well, will give an added dimension to the design.

A week before the wedding, the florist should prepare a buying list of the flowers and foliage needed (*Fig. 4.8*). Special flowers should be ordered well in advance from the wholesaler to ensure delivery.

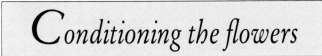

Fig. 4.8   Buying list

Always specify variety names and the quantities needed. **It is easy to overbuy, and a carefully thought out list will avoid this.** The flowers should arrive approximately two days before the wedding, which will give time for conditioning.

Always buy top quality flowers and foliage. Flowers are graded for quality, and the best quality ones usually last the longest. It is a mistake to skimp on quality.

When the flowers arrive at the shop, check the order carefully. Look at the quality of the flowers and note any breakages or short counts. Take action to ensure the wholesaler knows immediately.

Conditioning the flowers

On arrival, the flowers should be carefully conditioned as soon as possible. How the flowers are treated now will determine their lasting qualities. Some flowers may need specialised treatment, depending on the cell structure of the stem.

Conditioning tips

1 Always use a sharp knife. Cut the stems obliquely to ensure maximum water intake.

2 Give all the flowers plenty of fresh water in clean containers.

3 Do not cram too many flowers into each container. Allow space for the flowers to breathe.

4 Some foliage will benefit from being immersed in water.

5 In cold weather, flowers will respond more quickly if placed in tepid water.

6 To prevent premature ageing, remove all leaves that will be below the water line.

7 Always use a flower preservative in the water.

Take care when unpacking flowers to guard against breakages. Any broken flowers can be used for buttonholes or corsages. **Do not throw anything away.**

Once the conditioning has been completed, the flowers will need a period of time to revive before use. Ideally this should be in a cold room, dry cellar, or cool, dark, draught-free area.

Never use flowers that have not been properly conditioned.

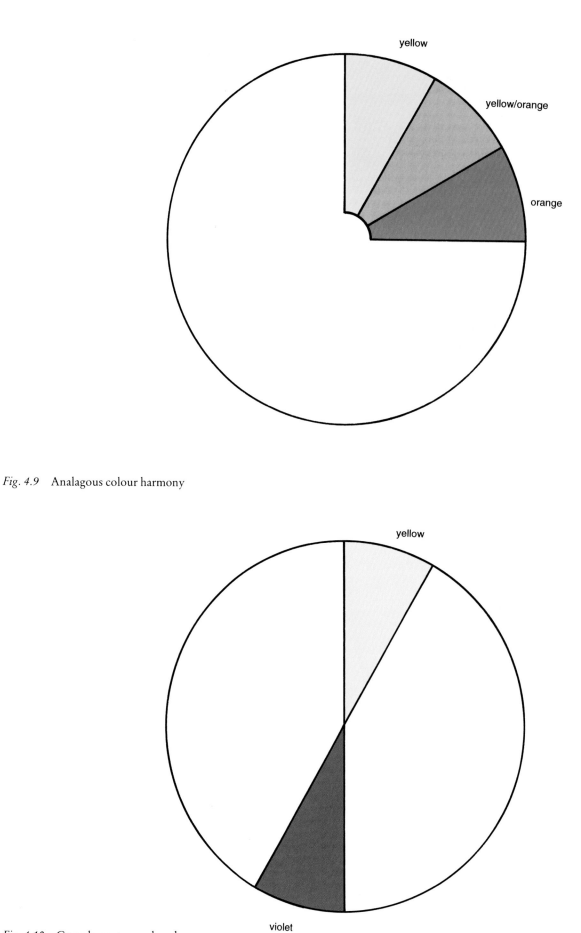

Fig. 4.9   Analagous colour harmony

Fig. 4.10   Complementary colour harmony

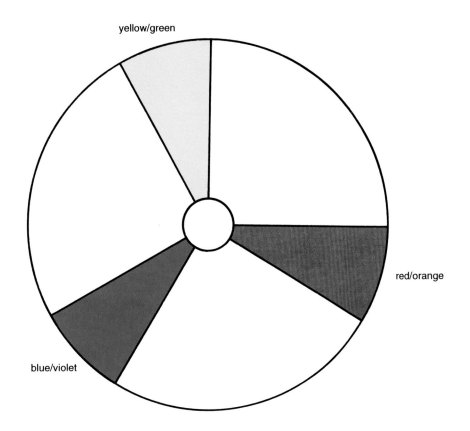

Fig. 4.11   Triadic colour harmony

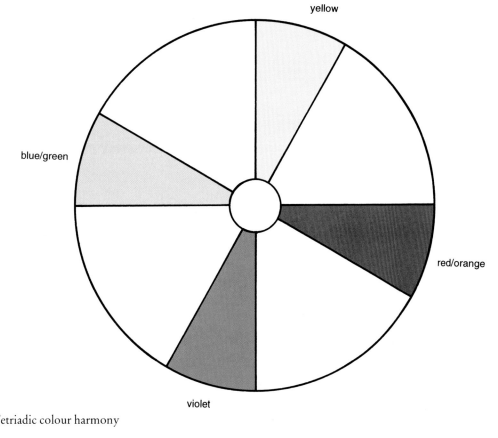

Fig. 4.12   Tetriadic colour harmony

The language of flowers

Although this secret art evolved in the harems of the Far East, the Victorians made the language of flowers their own. Each flower took on specific meaning and whole messages could be conveyed through them. Some flowers have symbolic meanings, used long before Victorian times to bring good fortune or ward off evil spirits.

Even today brides may ask for flowers and foliage which have special connotations. Some of the most popular flowers and their meanings are given in the following list.

Acacia	Friendship
Chrysanthemum (white)	Truth
Cinnamon	But my fortune is yours
Clematis	Mental beauty
Daffodil	Regard
Erica (white heather)	Good luck
Fern	Fascination
Forget me not	True love, forget me not
Golden rod	Precaution
Honesty	Honesty
Honey suckle	Devoted affection, generous
Hydrangea	Heartlessness
Ivy (hedera)	Mixed feelings. Some regard it as unlucky although used to ward off evil spirits. Used as a magic charm for love-lorn girls. Also means fidelity
Jasmine	Amiability
Jonquil	Have pity on my passion
Lily of the valley	Return to happiness
Lily white	Purity
Michaelmas daisy	Farewell

Myrtle	Evergreen shrub sacred to Venus, the goddess of love and lovers. Used in all royal wedding bouquets – taken off a shrub grown on the Isle of Wight from a cutting from Queen Victoria's wedding bouquet
Orange blossom	Prolific fruit, another sign of fertility
Orchid	Aphrodisiac
Pansy	Thoughts
Rosemary	Evergreen shrub. For remembrance
Roses	
– red	Most enduring symbol of true love
– white	I am worthy of you
– yellow	Jealousy
Stocks	Lasting beauty
Sweet pea	Delicate pleasure
Sweet william	Gallantry
Wheat/Corn	Fertility

Introduction

Buttonholes are a modern version of a wedding favour. Favours started in the 17th century when flowers tied with ribbons of various hues were given to all the guests at a wedding. The flowers were often selected for their symbolic meaning. Many flower varieties were worn by gentlemen, but the most popular became the carnation. White carnations were generally worn at weddings, surrounded by copious amounts of asparagus fern, with the stem wrapped in silver paper.

Today it is rare for all the male guests to be given buttonholes. Generally, only the immediate wedding party's buttonholes are organised by the bride:

- Bridegroom
- Best man
- Ushers
- Bride's father
- Bridegroom's father

Traditionally, men wear white for evening dress and morning dress (top hat and tails), and crimson for dinner jackets and formal day-wear (black jacket and pin-striped trousers). Nowadays, however, the bride will generally choose a colour for the buttonholes to complement her overall colour theme. Carnation buttonholes remain the traditional favourite, but they are worn mainly without foliage. Rose buttonholes are a smart alternative and gaining in popularity.

A boutonnière is a good way to link the bride and bridegroom's flowers. This is a special buttonhole made with flowers of the same variety as carried by the bride. Several small flowers can be used and the overall effect unites the bride and groom.

When choosing flowers for buttonholes, the lasting qualities of the bloom must be taken into consideration. A flower that wilts rapidly will look unsightly. All flowers must be well conditioned, and most foliage will benefit from being submerged in water for a short while. This will ensure the leaves stay turgid for longer.

Only perfect flowers without any blemishes should be used for buttonholes. Good workmanship and neat finish are essential ingredients for all buttonhole work. Make sure that the stem end of any buttonhole is finished off without any wire protruding. Always present buttonholes with a pin.

Carnation buttonhole

MATERIALS

1 carnation
Foliage if required (e.g. fern or similar)
0.90 mm × 180 mm stub wire
Several 0.32 mm silver rose wires
Small piece of silver binding wire
Tape
25 mm (1") pin

METHOD

1 Take a perfect, good-shaped carnation that has been well conditioned. Cut the stem, leaving approximately 15 mm ($\frac{1}{2}$") below the calyx.

2 Insert a 0.90 mm stub wire into the base of the stem and push it carefully through the flower.

3 Make a neat hook at the top of the wire and pull it carefully back through the flower until the hook nestles in the calyx (*Fig. 5.1*).

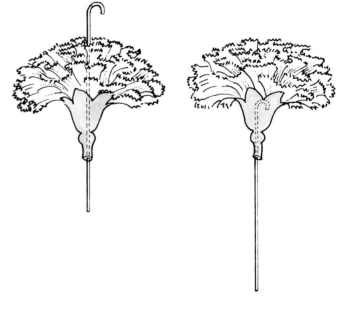

Fig. 5.1

4 Tape down the wire from the top of the stem.

5 If foliage is desired, wire three pieces of fern or similar with silver rose wires, using the single-leg method. One piece of foliage should be larger. Use restraint when adding foliage – it is there to complement not to overpower the flower.

Plate 7 Boutonnière

Plate 4 Gentleman's carnation buttonhole

Plate 6   Lady's rose buttonhole

Plate 5   Gentleman's rose buttonhole

6 Place the largest piece of foliage at the back of the flower. Arrange the two smaller pieces at the sides, towards the front of the carnation. Secure them together firmly with a small piece of silver binding wire around the top of the carnation stem.

7 Trim the wires to approximately 50 mm (2″) to form the stem. Tape them firmly and neatly down the stem, ensuring that all wiring is concealed. Finish off the stem end so that no wire protrudes.

8 Face the carnation by tilting the flower head slightly forwards.

9 Spray the buttonhole with water and add a 25 mm (1″) pin.

See Plate 4

Rose buttonhole

MATERIALS

1 rose
3–5 rose or hedera leaves
0.71 mm × 180 mm stub wire
Several silver rose wires
Small piece of binding wire
Tape
25 mm (1″) pin

METHOD

1 Choose a perfect rose which has been well conditioned. Cut the stem, leaving approximately 15 mm ($\frac{1}{2}$″) below the calyx. Remove any guard petals if necessary.

2 It may be necessary to pin through the sepals into the calyx with fine hairpins. Make these from silver rose wire. Only pin if the rose variety has a tendency to blow, or on very hot days.

3 Push a 0.71 mm stub wire up the stem into the seed box. Use a silver rose wire and push through the calyx, bringing the wires down either side of the stem (*Fig. 5.2*). This wire will give added security. Tape down the wire from the top of the stem.

4 Although the rose buttonhole will look more natural with its own foliage, this does have a tendency to wilt rapidly. Using two rose leaves together will aid longevity. Alternatively, small hedera leaves can give a pleasing effect. Use the stitch method to wire up three to five leaves (depending on the size of the rose), then tape down the wire stems.

5 Use the largest leaf at the back of the flower and arrange the other leaves at the sides. One leaf should be added to the front of the rose, bending it forwards over the stem (*Fig. 5.3*).

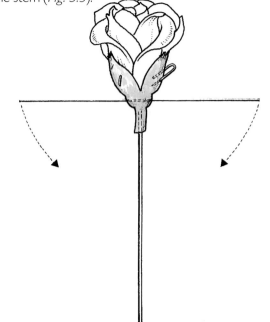

Fig. 5.2 Push silver rose wire through calyx, bringing wires down either side of stem

Fig. 5.3 Arrange leaves around rose

6 Secure all the leaves to the rose with a small amount of silver binding wire around the top of the rose stem.

7 Cut and taper the wires to approximately 50 mm (2″), to form the stem. Tape them firmly and neatly down the stem, ensuring all the wiring is concealed. Finish off the stem end so that no wire protrudes.

8 Face the rose by tilting the flower head slightly forwards.

9 Spray the buttonhole lightly with water and add a 25 mm (1″) pin.

See Plate 5

The rose buttonhole can also be suitable for a lady to wear – especially with the addition of a small bunch of gypsophila (or similar) and a bow of ribbon in a colour to complement the rose.

See Plate 6

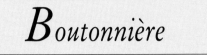

*B*outonnière

MATERIALS

2 stephanotis pips
1 small rose
2 hedera leaves
1 *Peperomia caperata* leaf
Bear grass
Wires, various gauges
Tape
25 mm (1") pin

METHOD

1 Select perfect flowers and foliage which have been well conditioned.

2 Wire and mount the stephanotis pips. Wire the rose and the leaves. Take two strands of bear grass, approximately 100 mm (4") in length, and make a unit of them. Also loop together another two strands of bear grass and wire. Once the wiring is complete, tape all the stems.

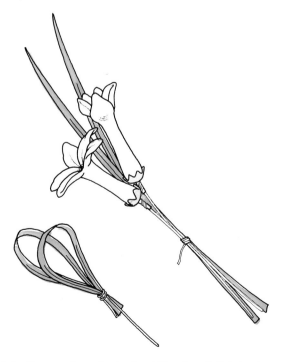

Fig. 5.4   One stephanotis pip should be placed slightly above the other

3 Take the unit of bear grass and the stephanotis pips. Arrange them together with one stephanotis pip slightly above the other, holding the wires at the binding point (*Fig. 5.4*).

4 Add the rose low into the focal area, in front of the stephanotis. Place the bear grass loops to one side of the rose (*Fig. 5.5*).

Fig. 5.5

5 Surround the flowers with the three leaves, then bind all the stems together just below the focal flower.

6 Trim and taper the wires, leaving approximately 50 mm (2"). Tape them firmly and neatly down the stem from the binding point, ensuring all the wiring is concealed. Finish off the stem end so that no wires protrude.

7 Spray the boutonnière with water and add a 25 mm (1") pin.

See Plate 7

*I*ntroduction

A corsage worn by a lady can be a single flower decorated with accessories such as ribbons or foliage, or a more complicated design using a variety of flowers and foliage. For the creative florist, it is an area which has no boundaries. Superb styles can be produced with very little flower material. Not every customer wants the same style or shape, and with a little imagination it can be fun experimenting with different designs. The reputation of your shop will be enhanced by using exciting variations and combinations of styles and flowers. It is good economy to use flowers left over from wedding bouquets and similar, which can be ideal for delicate corsages.

It is essential to design the corsage to complement the wearer, her dress and size. The style, colour, and texture of the material, and the whole ensemble, must all be taken into consideration when designing the corsage.

Most principal female guests will want to wear some form of body flowers. A corsage does not always have to be worn on the lapel. It can be used on the shoe, waist, shoulder or other parts of the anatomy. A corsage can also be fixed to a hat, handbag, parasol and other items of apparel. Many different shapes can be used for the design.

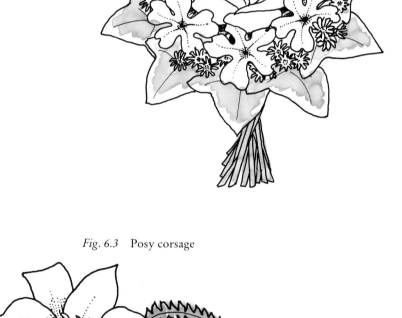

Fig. 6.3 Posy corsage

Fig. 6.1 Semi-crescent corsage

Fig. 6.2 Crescent corsage

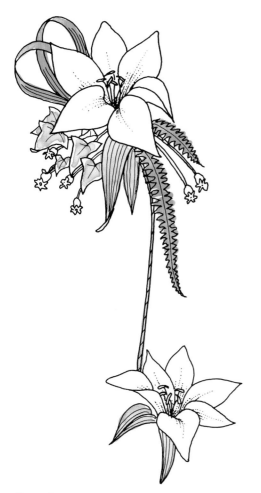

Fig. 6.4 Extension corsage

Fig. 6.5 Triangle corsage

Fig. 6.6 Hogarth curve corsage

Technically the workmanship must be impeccable. The corsage should be as light as a feather and well balanced so that it will sit perfectly on the wearer and not pull the fabric when attached. The wires should be covered to prevent damage. The flowers and foliage must be perfect and well conditioned.

When the corsage is completed, it is worthwhile spending a few moments to consider the way it will be presented to the customer. Even the humble buttonhole can be enhanced by its presentation. It also shows the customer your professionalism and care when the corsage or buttonhole is displayed well. It takes very little time and money to wrap the corsage in cellophane, trimmed with ribbon and your shop's name, but the visual appeal will be greatly enhanced.

A corsage is often given as a gift, and this will need a special presentation. A small acetate box is ideal to use. Crumple a small piece of damp tissue paper and place it in the bottom of the box to provide a bed for the corsage to sit on. Replace the lid and trim with ribbons to complement the colour of the corsage.

Traditional corsage

MATERIALS

2 units of small hedera leaves
2 units of 2 small arachnis or dendrobium
2 roses
5 small pieces of statice or similar
5 arachnis or dendrobium
6 hedera leaves
3 *Peperomia caperata* leaves or similar
2 dizygotheca leaves or similar
(These flowers and foliage can be substituted for similar sized material.)
2 groups of short bear grass, wired
Wires, various gauges
Reel wire
Tape
25 mm (1") pearl-headed pin

METHOD

1 Make sure the flowers and foliage chosen are all perfect and have been well conditioned. Wire and tape all the materials using the finest wires possible.

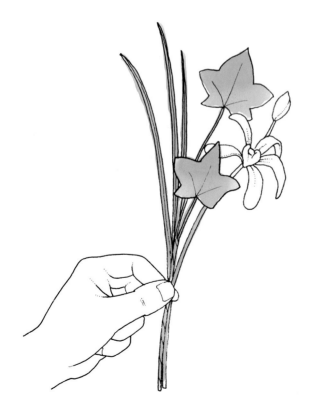

Fig. 6.7   Hold wire stems at focal point

2 Take a unit of small hedera leaves, a group of bear grass and a unit of arachnis. Arrange them together, holding the wire stems at the point where the focal area will be (*Fig. 6.7*).

3 Add more foliage and flowers to the outline, gradually increasing the width of the corsage.

4 Place a peperomia leaf and the smallest rose just above the binding point. Position an arachnis on one side of the rose and statice on the other side. Still holding all the stems together, arrange and bind them with reel wire at the focal area (*Fig. 6.8*).

Fig. 6.8

5 Add the focal rose above the binding point. Add hedera and flowers for width at the outline. This should be the widest part of the corsage. Use peperomia leaves around the focal rose for emphasis. Fill in with pieces of statice. Loops of bear grass can also be added for interest.

Keep the binding point in one place.

6 Take one unit of hedera leaves and one unit of arachnis. Place these units below the central rose, then bend them back over the stem to produce the return end of the corsage. Add other materials, where necessary, to the sides and bind them into the same position (*Fig. 6.9*).

Fig. 6.9 Slide return end under focal rose

Take care not to clutter the design with too many flowers.

7 Once the corsage is finished, a leaf can be added to the back of the corsage to hide the wiring. Trim off the wires to form a neat stem. Do not cut this stem too short – it should be slender and tapering, not a thick stump.

8 Tape from the top of the stem, concealing all the wiring. Finish the end of the stem neatly, ensuring no wires protrude.

9 Spray the corsage lightly with water.

10 Add a 25 mm (1″) pearl-headed pin.

See Plate 8

*M*odern corsage

A corsage using one bold flower with accessories can be both dramatic and stylish. Flowers such as small lilies, gerbera or cymbidium orchids are ideal for this. Teamed with a selection of interesting foliage, seed heads or other materials, it has immediate impact. For the person wishing to make a fashion statement, this modern style is perfect.

1 small lily head
2 lily buds, one smaller than the other
Bear grass
Selection of decorative foliage
Sedum or similar
4 small pieces of limonium
Wires, various gauges
Green binding wire
Tape
25 mm (1″) pin

METHOD

1 Select the foliage for its shape and texture, including hedera or similar round leaves. Choose flowers and foliage without blemishes that have been well conditioned. Remove the stamens from the open lily.

2 Wire all the flowers and foliage with the finest wires suitable. Leave the lily buds on 15 mm ($\frac{1}{2}$″) stems and wire each internally with a 0.56 mm wire (*Fig. 6.10*). Tape the end of the stem and continue down the wire. Push a 0.71 mm wire up the stem of the open lily, leaving 15 mm ($\frac{1}{2}$″) of stem. Take a silver rose wire through the base of the lily, bringing the wire down either side of the stem (*Fig. 6.11*). Make small bunches of sedum and wire them on 0.38 mm single-leg wires. Tape all the wires. Wire and tape all the foliage.

Fig. 6.10 Leave lily bud on 15 mm stem and wire internally

Plate 9 Modern corsage

Plate 8 Traditional corsage

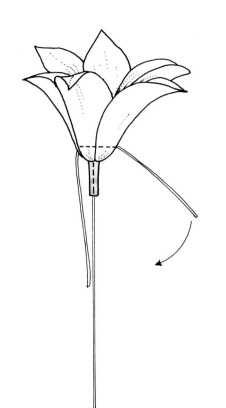

3 Take a group of long bear grass and add the two lily buds (one shorter than the other), one piece of limonium, a hedera leaf and a piece of sedum. Holding these together at the focal point, arrange them in a pleasing design. Bind them in one place with a fine reel wire (*Fig. 6.12*).

4 Place the open lily in the centre, tilting the head upwards slightly. Use larger hedera leaves surrounding the open lily, adding more line foliage and limonium in pleasing patterns through the corsage. Fill in with sedum. Bind all the materials into position (*Fig. 6.13*).

Keep the binding point in one place. Do not travel down the stem with the reel wire.

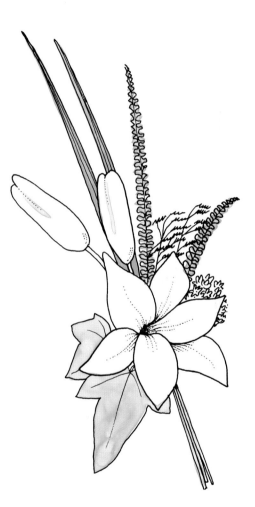

Fig. 6.11 Take silver rose wire through base of lily, bringing wire down either side of stem

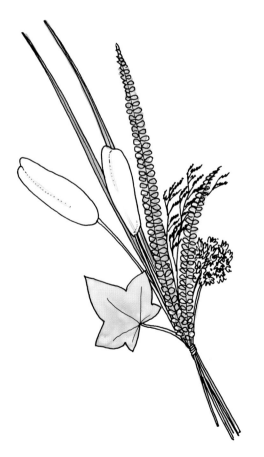

Fig. 6.13 Place open lily above binding point

5 Select three strands of fine bear grass and wire both ends of the group. Attach one end to one side of the corsage and loop the bear grass over the corsage to the other side. Bind it into place with reel wire. Another unit of bear grass can be used in a similar fashion, placing this loop towards the return end of the corsage (*Fig. 6.14*).

Fig. 6.12 Assemble, holding stems together at binding point

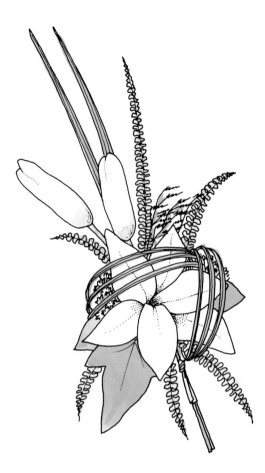

Fig. 6.14   Loop bear grass over corsage

6 When the corsage is finished, use one hedera leaf at the back of the corsage to conceal the wiring and finish the design. Trim off the wires to form a neat stem. Do not cut the stem too short – it should be slender and tapering, not a thick stump.

7 Tape from the top of the stem, concealing all the wiring. Finish the stem end neatly, ensuring no wires protrude.

8 Spray the corsage lightly with water.

9 Add a 25 mm (1″) pearl-headed pin.

See Plate 9

This type of corsage can look stunning as a hat decoration, sewn neatly in place at the base of the crown. Never use glue on a hat as this could cause damage. Careful sewing with a few large stitches will anchor the corsage firmly to the hat. Never sew onto the brim of a hat as this will pull it out of shape.

A corsage can be easily adapted to form a wrist spray. This can be offered as an alternative, particularly for someone who is disabled and needs the use of both hands. The corsage can be tied to the wrist with ribbons, or attached to a bracelet of covered wire.

*H*andbag decoration

A handbag decoration can be a useful alternative to a corsage, particularly when the dress worn is heavily patterned or multi-coloured, or when the fabric is very flimsy. Decorations for the handbag may be chosen by brides wearing day-wear at informal weddings, by brides' mothers and principal guests at weddings.

The style of the handbag will dictate the type of design and the method of attachment. The design of the corsage should be made to complement the size of the handbag and should not completely cover it. When securing the corsage, never sew, glue, pin, or use adhesive tape. This will cause damage to the handbag. It should also be possible to open the handbag without dislodging the corsage.

Always ask the customer to bring in the handbag a few days before the wedding, and attach the design in the shop. A clutch bag is the most popular type of handbag carried at a wedding.

When designing the corsage, remember that the handbag is often carried below waist height. Design the corsage to look good from the front and from above. The corsage should be fairly flat – any flowers and foliage that protrude will be in danger of damage.

MATERIALS

1 Solidago stem
2 small buds and 3 open single chrysanthemum heads
9 small- to medium-sized hedera leaves
7 *Codiaeum variegatum* 'Gold Star' leaves
Tape
Wires, various gauges
2.90 mm × 300 mm (12″) stub wires, taped together
The corsage described is designed for a clutch bag, approximate size 255 mm (10″) × 150 mm (6″)

METHOD

1 Choose the materials carefully for their shape and lasting qualities. Ensure the flowers and foliage complement the colour and texture of the handbag, and the gown worn.

2 After the flowers and foliage have been well conditioned, wire and tape them using the finest wires possible. Wire three codiaeum leaves into loops, and wire the chrysanthemum and solidago using the method shown (*Fig. 6.15*).

4 Add a small hedera leaf and bud chrysanthemum, and gradually increase the width of the corsage with foliage and flowers. Keep trying the corsage on the handbag for perfect proportions. Bind all the flowers and foliage together at the focal point, using a small length of fine binding wire. The widest part of the corsage should be at the focal area.

5 The focal flower – the largest chrysanthemum head – should be positioned next, at the centre of the corsage. Fill in with solidago, codiaeum loops and hedera leaves. Another head of chrysanthemum should be placed just below the focal flower. (*See Fig. 6.17.*)

Fig. 6.15

3 Start to assemble the corsage. Take a unit of solidago and one codiaeum leaf. Arrange them together, holding the stems at the focal area (*see Fig. 6.16*).

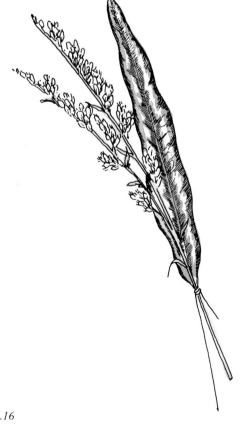

Fig. 6.16

Fig. 6.17

6 Before starting the return end, tuck a hedera leaf beneath the focal flower and bend it back over the stem to hide the mechanics. Then use a unit of solidago, a codiaeum leaf, chrysanthemum bud and hedera leaf and arrange them to form the return end. Slot this unit in below the focal flower and bind it in, then pull it back over the stem. Fill in the sides of the corsage where necessary.

7 Once the corsage has been completed satisfactorily, trim and taper the stem end.

8 Take the long taped wires. Position the corsage at the centre of the wire so that the same amount of wire is visible at both ends of the corsage. Tape the wire to the stem at one end, and secure the wire to the other end of the corsage by taping it neatly to the first unit. The wire and the corsage should now be firmly joined in two places.

9 Spray the corsage with water. Do not spray it when attached to the handbag as the water could cause damage.

10 Place the corsage on the handbag at the best angle. Remember that a more interesting effect may be obtained by placing it diagonally rather than horizontally. Bend the stay wires firmly inside the flap of the bag at either side to secure the corsage to the handbag. The tape on the stay wire should be concealed by the corsage. The tape should be of a similar colour to the handbag, to be as unobtrusive as possible. (*See Fig. 6.18.*)

Fig. 6.18

Introduction

Brides have always adorned their hair with flowers and this tradition continues today, with fresh flower headdresses consistently popular at weddings.

Above all, floral headdresses capture the romance of the day. When made with a medley of the season's flowers entwined with vines, or aromatic herbs embellished with tiny sea shells, the headdress will reproduce the magical aura of old-fashioned nuptials.

Garlands or circlets of flowers and alice bands are the most popular styles for all age groups. However, there are many other designs that can be created, and the florist should be able to tailor any fashion to complement the hairstyle worn and the bouquet carried.

How the hair is to be worn will dictate the style of the headdress. A particularly pleasing effect will be obtained by carrying through the theme, linking the bouquet to the headdress in colour, content of flower material and style. Both headdress and bouquet should complement the gown worn. A complete image is created when the wedding bouquet and headdress are co-ordinated.

Whatever the style, certain technical requirements must be achieved. The comfort of the wearer is of prime concern. The headdress must therefore be light in weight, fit perfectly and have firm anchorage. Many hairdressers complain that insufficient thought is given by the florist as to how the headdress will stay in place on the head. A method of anchorage must be included. Loops of covered wire can be easily added to the headdress during assembly. Circlets, alice bands and side sprays should all have firm anchorage loops. **However lovely the headdress, it will be useless if there is no method of fixing attached.**

Make sure all the wires are covered so that none can cause damage to the head or veil.

Choose flowers and foliage for their durability. One-third of body heat is emitted from the head, therefore flowers and foliage that wilt rapidly are not suitable.

Careful workmanship and neat construction are essential as the headdress will be seen from every angle and at eye level. Measurements should always be taken, particularly when making a circlet or alice band. When assembling, keep trying the headdress in the position it will be worn. Look at it from various aspects to ensure maximum impact whichever way it is viewed.

Headdress styles

Garland/circlet

This is a very popular style for both brides and their attendants. The garland or circlet is a band of flowers and foliage made to form a circle. It can be made with many different types of flowers and foliage, and in varying widths according to the volume and style of hair. It is a very pretty style for small bridesmaids. (The garland headdress is discussed in more detail on page 38.)

See Plate 10

Alice band

The alice band is a semicircle of flowers which can be worn in many ways, as a brow band or on the top or back of the head. Ribbon streamers can be added to the ends of the band to give a peasant-style headdress.

See Plate 11

Comb

Single flowers or corsage-style designs can be securely fastened to a comb. Many different types of designs can be made in this way. (The comb headdress is discussed in more detail on page 42.)

See Plate 12

Tiara

The tiara is a semicircle of flowers, with several upright units of flowers or one central upright spray. Pearls and other beads can be added (*Fig. 7.1*).

Coronet

The coronet resembles a small crown and is generally worn only by the bride. It consists of a small circle of flowers worn on the top of the head, with seven or eight upright units (*Fig. 7.2*). It is a fairytale headdress which is most suitable when worn with a romantic-style wedding gown. Gold and silver threads or diamante can be added to achieve the desired ethereal effect.

Fig. 7.1   Tiara headdress

Fig. 7.2   Coronet headdress

*G*arland headdress

A garland or circlet headdress can be made to any width, from a narrow band of tiny chincherinchee to a wild, country style of full-blown roses. Consider the volume of hair and the size of the bride's face when deciding on the width of the headdress. Too heavy a design will be unsuitable for a tiny face.

Always measure the head to ensure the correct fit. An adult's garland will measure approximately 500 mm (20″). If the measurements are not available, always make a hook and eye at the ends of the foundation wire so that the headdress can be altered if necessary.

The foundation wire should be firm and moulded to the shape of the head. Millinery wire is ideal, as this comes on a roll and can be cut to the exact measurements. If the foundation wire is too fine, the headdress will not hold its shape or sit comfortably on the head.

An alternative to a full garland is an alice band. This is a half circle of flowers, generally placed over the top of the head, with flowers extending from ear to ear. The approximate length of an alice band for an adult is 250 mm (10″). The alice band can look lovely if worn on the back of the head or as a brow band. It can be designed to be wider in the centre, tapering to the sides, or the same width throughout. There are many different styles of headdress that can be achieved using a semicircular foundation wire.

Choose an interesting mixture of flowers and foliage, of varying shapes. Do not dismiss seed heads, dried grasses and exotic materials. A length of millinery wire as a foundation, complete with anchorage loops, will be easier to fix into the hair than manufactured alice bands with no methods of attachment. These will easily fall out once the weight of the flowers is added to them.

MATERIALS

525 mm (21″) length of millinery wire (or correct length for head plus 25 mm (1″) for overlapping)
28 small- and medium-sized hedera leaves
36 spray rose heads, buds and open flowers
36 small bunches of september, *Alchemilla mollis*, gypsophila or similar
22 small bunches of hypericum or small seed heads
36 pieces of *Eryngium planum*
12 small pieces of statice
Tape
Wires, various gauges

METHOD

1 Form the foundation wire to the shape of the head (overlapping the wire slightly) then join the ends together firmly, taping the whole circle. If unsure of the size of the head, make a hook and eye at the ends of the wire (*Fig. 7.3*).

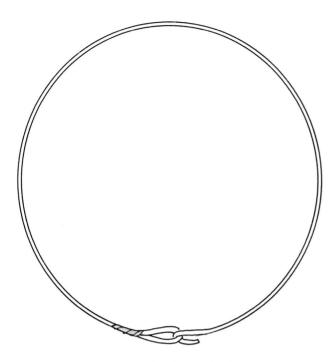

Fig. 7.3 If unsure of size of head, make hook and eye at ends of wire

2 Tape four 0.56 mm × 75 mm wires and bend them to form loops. These will be added underneath the garland as anchorage loops (*Fig. 7.4*).

Fig. 7.4 Add anchorage loops to garland

3 Choose best quality flowers and foliage which have been well conditioned. Give consideration to the lasting qualities of the flowers.

4 Wire and tape all the flowers and foliage using the finest wires possible. Wire the september, hypericum, statice and eryngium in small bunches on 0.38 mm silver wires, using the single-leg method.

5 Start assembling the headdress by lying the flowers and foliage in close formation on top of the foundation wire (ribbed-unit style). Working around the circle, group the flowers and foliage to make pleasing patterns, overlapping each one slightly and rolling materials to either side to give a rounded appearance.

6 As the headdress progresses, tape all the materials firmly to the foundation wire, cutting out unnecessary wires to keep the headdress light and neat (*Fig. 7.5*).

Fig. 7.5 Tape all materials firmly to foundation wire, cutting out unnecessary wires

7 As the end of the circle is reached, make sure that the materials are tucked underneath the first flowers. This will ensure a continuous ring of flowers and foliage, with no visible start or finish.

8 Alternatively, the garland can be finished off with a bow or ribbon and streamers.

9 Spray the garland lightly with water. Sit it on a bed of damp tissue paper and enclose in a sealed polythene bag until packaging the wedding order.

See Plate 10

Plate 10   Garland/circlet headdress

Plate 11 Alice band

Comb headdress

A headdress made on a comb can be a very simple style using a few flowers or an elaborate design of mixed flowers and foliage. It can be quick and easy to make, using flowers left over from other bridal work.

The comb headdress can be worn in any position on the head. It is therefore important to discuss with the bride, or bridesmaid, where it is to be worn, and to design it accordingly.

Use a comb which is bevelled to the contours of the head and has long teeth for firm anchorage. Anchorage loops should also be attached for extra safety.

The headdress shown in **Plate 12** has trails of foliage and flowers which tumble downwards, mingling with the hair. It is worn towards the top of the head at one side.

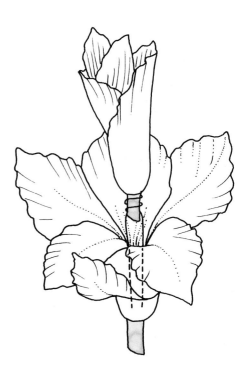

MATERIALS

2 small hedera trails
6–10 hedera leaves or similar
5 gladioli pips (buds)
2 open gladioli
6 cordyline (red edge) leaves or similar
Several small sprigs of statice
Bear grass
Wires, various gauges
Tape
Reel of binding wire

METHOD

1 Choose perfect flowers which have been well conditioned.

2 Wire all the foliage using the stitch method. Group and wire together the strands of bear grass. Wire several small sprigs of statice. Tape all the wires.

3 Wire the gladioli buds on 0.38 mm wires, using the single-leg method.

4 Make two double gladioli flowers. To do this, take one of the bud gladioli pips which is already wired. Push the bud down the throat of the open gladioli, with the wires coming out through the base of the open flower. Take a 0.32 mm silver wire and push it straight through the base of the open flower and bud. Wire using the double-leg method, then tape from the base of the flower (*Fig. 7.6*). Mount onto a 0.56 mm or 0.71 mm wire, depending on the weight of the flower.

Fig. 7.6 Gladioli double flower

5 Once all the flowers and foliage have been wired and taped, start to assemble the headdress. Arrange together a trail of hedera, a group of long bear grass and a unit of gladioli pips, holding them at the binding point. Then place a unit of cordyline and a unit of hedera either side of the main trails. A hedera leaf in the centre will cover the mechanics (*Fig. 7.7*).

Fig. 7.7

6 Place a double gladioli flower in the centre of the design. Bind all the stems together below the central flower.

7 Add width to the focal area with groups of statice and foliage. Use cordyline leaves grouped through the design.

8 Bend the design as it is being made, to fit the contours of the head. Try the headdress in position as it is assembled.

9 Use some foliage and statice recessed below the focal flower.

10 Place the other double gladioli flower into the return end, with a small trail of hedera, a group of bear grass and a lily bud. Bend them into place.

11 Fill in to ensure all the mechanics are concealed and the design looks good from all angles (*Fig. 7.8*).

12 Add two anchorage loops to the back of the headdress. Cut and taper the wires to the length of the comb. Tape the stem, ensuring all wires are covered.

13 Attach the headdress securely to the comb with glue or a covered wire (*Fig. 7.9*).

14 Spray the headdress with water and cover with polythene until required.

See Plate 12

Fig. 7.8 Ensure design looks good from all angles

Fig. 7.9 Attach headdress to comb with covered wire

Plate 12   Comb headdress

*B*ouquet styles

*V*ictorian posy

In a Victorian posy, the flowers are arranged tightly in concentric circles around a focal flower and edged and finished with leaves or a frill. Ribbon streamers can also be added. A slightly domed top is usual. This style is more interesting when a variety of different-shaped flowers and foliage are used. Seed heads, beads, mosses and fruits can all be used to create a more exciting design.

See Plate 13

*L*oose/*E*dwardian posy

The loose or Edwardian posy has a circular outline which is loose in style and broken by spiky materials. This style is again more interesting when made of a variety of different-shaped flowers. The posy is slightly domed. Materials are placed at varying levels within the design to create depth and interest. (The loose posy is discussed in more detail on page 47.)

See Plate 14

*S*hower bouquet

The shower bouquet has a classic, symmetrical design, with softly cascading flowers coming from a central point. Many variations of this style can be made, such as the curved shower. Generally, the flowers are loosely arranged within the symmetrical shape. Grouping of flowers through the bouquet strengthens the visual appeal. This is the most popular style of bouquet for brides. (The shower bouquet is discussed in more detail on page 51.)

See Plate 15

*C*rescent bouquet

The crescent bouquet is based on one-third of a circle (*Fig. 8.1*). Materials flow from a central point, with each side of the bouquet mirroring the other. To achieve the elegant, softly curved effect, choose flowers and foliage which have a natural sweeping form. This is a suitable style if the bride has a heavily patterned or embroidered front skirt panel. The crescent bouquet will complement without concealing the detail of the dress.

Fig. 8.1   Crescent bouquet

*S*emi-crescent bouquet

The semi-crescent bouquet is a very elegant style. The shape is based on two-thirds of a circle, with one elongated, sweeping side (*Fig. 8.2*). Balance is achieved by placing larger leaves and flowers (those with more visual weight) on the shorter side of the bouquet. Choose flowers and foliage which are naturally curving. Skilful choice of materials is essential to achieve this graceful style.

Fig. 8.2   Semi-crescent bouquet

Line bouquet

In the line bouquet, a group or line of one flower is most dominant. Generally, a bold flower such as a lily or rose is used for the main group. The shape of the bouquet will be determined by the flowers used. Restraint should be used with secondary groups of flowers and foliage, so that the dominant line is not cluttered. They should accentuate not detract from the main group. The minimum of materials should be used. The line bouquet is beautiful in its simplicity, particularly when carried against a straight, plain dress. (*See Fig. 8.3.*)

Fig. 8.4   Extension bouquet

Fig. 8.3   Line bouquet

Extension bouquet

For an extension bouquet, small corsage-type designs or single flowers are attached to wires, ribbons or twigs and suspended from the main bouquet. The extensions should be light in weight and clearly separated from the main bouquet, otherwise the design will look confused. This style of bouquet can be modern or traditional. (*See Fig. 8.4.*)

Continental bouquet

Continental is the name given to many styles of modern bouquet, in various forms; vegetative, experimental, free-form, etc. Generally, they are made in an upright style, with great emphasis on design and choice of material. Skilful use of mosses, fungi, seed heads and foliage, along with modern design techniques such as terracing and pillowing, will produce an exciting style. The continental bouquet can be carried by brides wearing a traditional long dress and is also ideal for modern, short day-wear. (The continental bouquet is discussed in more detail on page 55.)

See Plate 16

Waterfall bouquet

Reminiscent of the baroque style, the waterfall design is a cascade of tumbling materials starting from a central point. Long trailing materials overlay each other to achieve the desired 'untidy' look. The bouquet is generally made with small flowers and foliage such as vines and ferns to achieve the tumbling effect. Tiny beads or flowers can be tied to the foliage or onto extensions of wool, coloured wire or threads. The bouquet can be made in a hand-tied fashion, on a foam holder or using a traditional wired method. The whole effect of the bouquet should be of exuberance and extravagance. (*See Fig. 8.5.*)

Fig. 8.6   Tufted/textured bouquet

Fig. 8.5   Waterfall bouquet

Tufted/textured bouquet

For the tufted or textured bouquet, flowers and foliage are grouped in compact sections. Interesting shapes and textures are important. The solid groups can be broken by the use of line material (e.g. bear grass and twigs), to give movement to the tightly massed design. This style of bouquet can be made in a hand-tied construction, on a foam holder or using a traditional wired method. (*See Fig. 8.6.*)

Hand-tied bouquets are discussed on page 60.

Loose/Edwardian posy

A posy of flowers is the most enduring style for a bridal bouquet. In Victorian times the posy was made in solid bands of flowers, grouped tightly in concentric circles. A single flower was generally surrounded by four circles of flowers, then finished with a collar of leaves or a frill of lace. This was typical of the heavy Victorian style and, because the flower stems were weak, the tight binding kept the bouquet in place throughout the ceremony.

In Edwardian times, a more delicate posy emerged with flowers freely arranged within a circular outline. This is the posy that has become most popular with brides and their bridesmaids. One reason for its popularity is that it can be made to any size, and is therefore equally suitable for tiny bridesmaids and for the bride herself.

The posy is more interesting when a variety of flowers and foliage in different shapes are used. The materials should appear to radiate from a central point. Overcrowding must be avoided in any loose design, but this is particularly important in a circular shape where too many heavy, round flowers can produce a static, unnatural-looking design. The choice of materials is very important so that the right blend of shapes is achieved. Each flower should be seen with a space around it. Recessing some materials low into the design will give an attractive, three-dimensional appearance to the finished posy.

Plate 13 Victorian posy

Plate 14   Loose/Edwardian posy

WEDDING BOUQUETS

Whether the posy is made in a traditional wired method or on a foam holder, the principles of good design apply.

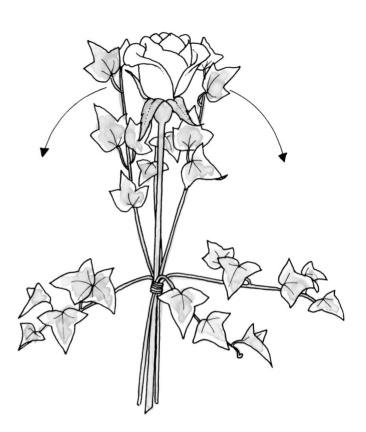

Fig. 8.7   Pull each hedera trail down to form circular outline

MATERIALS

4 roses
12 small pieces of acacia
12 small pieces of september or similar
10 sweet pea heads
5 freesia stems
35 brodiaea pips
2 spray carnation stems
10 short hedera trails
10 larger hedera leaves
10 short pieces of eucalyptus
Wires, various lengths and gauges
Tape
Fine reel wire
25 mm (1") satin ribbon

METHOD

1   Select all the flowers and foliage carefully. Only perfect blooms should be used. Remove the guard petals from the roses. Make sure that all the flowers and foliage have been well conditioned before use.

2   Wire and tape all the flowers and foliage correctly.

3   Make six branching units of brodiaea.

4   With all the materials carefully wired and neatly taped, the posy is ready for assembly.

5   Hold the focal rose in your hand and attach green-coated binding wire approximately 100 mm (4") to 125 mm (5") down the stem. This is now the binding point. **The binding wire must stay in this position and not travel down the stem.**

6   Make the circular outline by placing six hedera trails in an upright position around the focal flower. The tips of the hedera trails should be level with the top of the rose head. Bind them into place tightly, then pull each hedera trail down to form a horizontal circle around the focal flower (Fig. 8.7). This will determine the height and width of the posy.

7   All wires should be straight to form a neat handle. Do not twist or cross the stems.

8   Insert the other three roses at varying heights around the central rose (Fig. 8.8).

9   Place three or four larger hedera leaves low onto the binding point at the centre of the bouquet (Fig. 8.9).

Fig. 8.8   Insert three roses at varying heights around central rose

Fig. 8.9

10 Add two open heads of spray carnation, recessing them onto the ivy leaves to give a three-dimensional aspect to the posy.

11 Fill in the outline between the hedera trails with six units of brodiaea and sweet pea.

12 Next add five freesia stems and the rest of the brodiaea and sweet peas to the centre of the bouquet and fill in between the outer flowers and focal roses. Place the flowers at varying lengths for interest and take care not to overcrowd the design.

13 Make sure the binding point remains in the same position and does not travel down the stem.

14 The posy should be almost finished now. Use sprays of september, acacia and eucalyptus in and around the posy to give a light, delicate look. Add more leaves if necessary.

15 When the bouquet is completed to your satisfaction, add four or five leaves to the back of the bouquet to neaten and cover the wires.

16 Cut off the binding wire. Trim and taper the handle wires to approximately 100 mm (4–4½″) in length, then tape them firmly down the handle.

17 The handle is now ready for ribboning (see page 59). The handle ribbon should always match the flowers used in the posy. Only use white ribbon if white is the most dominant colour of flowers, otherwise the handle will become overpowering.

18 Spray the bouquet well with water. Cover and store it in a cool, dark area.

See Plate 14

Shower bouquet

Most brides desire a fairytale wedding, with all the trimmings that go with that dream. It includes carrying a luxuriant, cascading bouquet of sumptuous flowers and foliage. This is why the popularity of the shower bouquet never wains. It is the traditional style that goes with the romantic vision of a perfect day.

The shower bouquet is a symmetrical style. Within this classical outline, different styles can be achieved. A simple elegant shower of lilies with stephanotis and lily of the valley is perfect for the bride wearing a stylish, plain dress. A fuller, untidy garden style, using an abundance of trailing ivies and country flowers, will complement a pretty, full-skirted dress. Both styles use the same symmetrical shape. With clever use of colour and an eye for detail, you should be able to create an individual style for every wedding – never churning out the same bouquet for every bride.

The symmetrical shape is slightly rounded at the top, with trails of foliage and flowers cascading from a central point. Smaller flowers are generally used for the outline, gradually building in size to the largest flowers at the focal point. Grouping both flowers and foliage through the design will aid continuity and visual balance.

The size of the bouquet will be determined by the height of the bride and the style of dress. The bouquet should look in proportion with the bride. The bouquet is seen from all angles, so as much attention should be given to the profile as the frontal view. A flat bouquet will look unsightly, particularly in photographs which tend to magnify any design mistakes.

Whether using a foam holder or making a wired bouquet, construction should be fine and neat. The design should sit well in the hand without tipping. Drawing flowers and foliage back slightly over the

Plate 15 Shower bouquet

Plate 16   Continental bouquet

hand will aid balance and give a good profile. Use flowers and foliage on natural stems wherever possible. Some flowers and foliage may need discreet support wiring, particularly those used in vulnerable positions such as the outline and focal flowers. This should be as unobtrusive as possible. Use the lightest wires to keep the natural shape without appearing rigid.

MATERIALS

10 roses
2 lily stems (with some open flowers)
10 freesia stems
2 sweet pea bunches
5 spray rose stems
25 stephanotis pips
3 limonium stems or similar
Hedera trails
Bear grass
Selection of interesting foliage
Large leaves (e.g. hedera, cyclamen or similar)
Foam holder
Wires, various gauges
Glue gun and glue
Bouquet stand
Tape

METHOD

1 Select only perfect flowers and foliage which have been well conditioned. Remove any damaged guard petals from the roses and the stamens from the lilies.

2 Choose a foam holder. Always use a bouquet stand while making the design. Never place a bouquet directly onto a work bench as this will cause damage to the delicate blooms.

3 Wire the stephanotis pips and mount them into branching units.

4 Start by making the outline of the bouquet using the proportions shown in *Fig. 8.10*. Mount the trails of hedera onto 0.56 mm or 0.71 mm wires (depending on the weight of stem). Insert the stems into the foam holder by glueing or wiring them into position (see page 58). Build up the outline by grouping the foliage and gradually increasing the width. The widest part of the bouquet should be at the focal area. Continue making a rounded outline at the top of the bouquet. Use all the foam, placing outline foliage around the edges of the foam. **All stems must be firmly anchored into the foam.**

5 Use some foliage to give depth to the bouquet, and place larger leaves (hedera, cyclamen or similar) around the centre of the foam.

Fig. 8.10   Outline foliage

6 Group the flowers through the design, starting with the most prominent flowers; roses and lilies. Use the roses as the main central grouping, varying the length of stem, but leave space in the focal area for the open lilies.

Some flowers will need support wiring, particularly those on the outline and focal areas.

7 Add three open lilies to the centre of the bouquet. These focal flowers should be positioned in a direct line with the handle, to achieve actual balance (*Fig. 8.11*). Add the lily buds to either side of the open flowers, grouping them outwards to the outline of the bouquet (*Fig. 8.12*).

8 Add the freesia to one side of the main grouping, bringing them through to the top of the bouquet. Group the spray roses, stephanotis and sweet peas in a similar method at the sides of the bouquet.

Fig. 8.12 Placement of open lilies and buds

Fig. 8.11 Focal flowers should be positioned in a direct line with handle

9 Fill in the design with flowers and foliage, recessing some flowers right onto the foam. As you work, ensure the profile also has recession. It is easy to ruin the design by overuse of foliage to cover the foam. Moss pinned onto the foam conceals without cluttering the design.

10 Finish off the bouquet by checking that there is no foam showing, the design of the bouquet is pleasing and all flowers and foliage are securely anchored into the foam.

11 Insert a collar of large hedera leaves around the back of the bouquet holder for a neat finish. A bow can be glued to the holder if desired. Use a colour ribbon to tone with the flowers used.

12 Spray the bouquet well with water. Cover and place it in a cool place to rest before packaging.

See Plate 15

Continental bouquet

A continental bouquet can take many forms; experimental, formal linear or vegetative. Whichever form, there is more emphasis on design than in traditional massed bouquets. The continental bouquet is generally made in the upright style, with the handle emerging centrally below the bouquet. Materials are grouped around the central handle so that it is interesting to look at from all angles. This bouquet shows a move away from basic shapes to more original free-form styles.

The choice of materials is vitally important. Look for contrasting shapes and textures, and use the flower materials naturally as they grow. In traditional designs, the flower material is generally sweeping downwards; in this style, many flowers are used in upright positions. Foliage also plays an important role.

Before starting the bouquet, think about what shape and style the design should be. Conjure up a mental picture of the finished bouquet. Look around at the materials available. You may get inspiration from a stem of orchids gently bending downwards, or a twig twisting and curling upwards. The colour of a flower may also trigger an idea. Use the principles and elements of design as a guide.

It is often easier to make this type of bouquet in a traditional wired method. As there are fewer flowers and foliage to wire it can be very quick to make, and covering a large expanse of foam can be a problem when using a bouquet holder. With materials placed all around the central handle, balance should not be a problem. The bouquet should sit in the hand without tipping.

MATERIALS

5 *Asparagus sprengeri* trails
4 nephrolepsis leaves
4 croton leaves
I amaranthus stem
I lily stem (with some open flowers)
Berries or rose hips
6 roses
5 freesia stems
3 dendrobium stems
Variety of interesting foliage (e.g. hedera and fatsia)
Wires, various gauges
Tape
Reel wire
25 mm (1") ribbon for handle

METHOD

I Ensure all the flowers and foliage have been well conditioned and are perfect.

2 Gather the materials together in your hand. Try them in different positions to find the best sites.

3 Wire all the flowers and foliage. Use the finest wires possible for support, while still allowing natural movement. Most of the flowers should be left on their natural stems.

4 Start the bouquet by determining the height with two roses. Hold these where the binding point will be.

5 Group croton leaves, nephrolepsis fronds and hedera trails around the central roses to establish the width of the bouquet. Large leaves such as fatsia are important to give weight to the base of the design. Secure all the foliage into the binding point with reel wire (*Fig. 8.13*).

6 Add trailing foliage such as *Asparagus sprengeri* to flow downwards from the bouquet.

Fig. 8.13   Establish width and height of bouquet

7 Once the height and width have been obtained, use two roses at both the front and back of the bouquet to give a focal area. Two open lily heads should also be placed towards the central position (*Fig. 8.14*).

Fig. 8.14   Place roses and open lily heads in centre of bouquet

Plate 17 Foam holders

Always finish the bouquet with a collar of leaves at the back

8 Group freesia and dendrobium through the bouquet with berries or hips, recessed low into the bouquet. **The binding point must remain in one position.**

9 Fill in the design with interesting foliage, amaranthus and seed heads. Do not clutter the design.

10 Finish the underside of the bouquet with a collar of leaves.

11 Cut wires to form the handle (see page 59).

12 Spray the bouquet with water, cover it with polythene and leave it in a cool place until required.

See Plate 16

*F*oam holders

Over the years, there have been many forms of construction for wedding bouquets. In the 1940s, the flowers were wired on a single-mount wire, then each wire was pushed through a moss ball and bent to form a handle.

The traditional wired bouquet has been the most enduring method of construction. It can, however, be time consuming to make because of the high degree of wiring. This makes labour charges high and it is then difficult to keep costs down when the bride wants an economical bouquet. Foam holders can eliminate a lot of the tedious wiring, enabling bouquets to be made more quickly.

Foam holders can be bought in a variety of styles. **See Plate 17.** Some have a dry foam ball, others contain foam that is immersed in water before use. Whichever style the florist prefers, there are technical details to consider before using it.

Flowers and foliage must have secure anchorage into the foam. Wedding bouquets are handled many times during and after the ceremony. The most common complaint is that flowers fall out of the foam. There are two methods to obtain maximum security. One method is to mount the flower stems on single-leg mount wires. Each wire is then pushed right through the foam ball so that it protrudes for approximately 25 mm (1"). A hook is then made on the end of the wire and pushed back into the foam ball (*Fig. 8.15*). An alternative method is to glue the stem ends into the dry foam ball. The stem end is cut obliquely, a small amount of glue is added, and the stem is then pushed firmly into the foam ball.

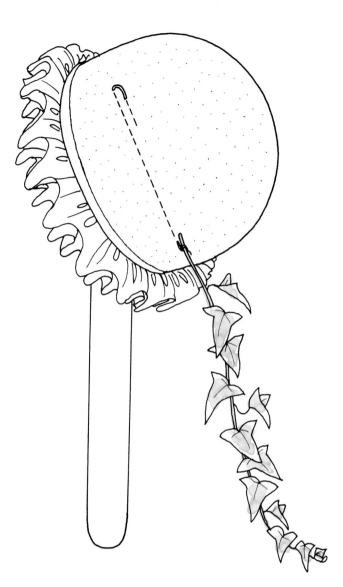

Fig. 8.15 Single-leg mount wire pushed through foam ball, then hooked back in for extra security

Use all the foam, placing the outline flowers and foliage around the base of the holder. This will eliminate unsightly exposed areas of foam. When the bouquet is finished, there should be no foam visible. Covering the foam can be a problem and over-use of fussy foliage can destroy the design. Try to mask the foam with larger flat leaves or moss placed flat onto the foam. The moss can be hairpinned or glued into place.

Always finish the bouquet with a collar of leaves at the back. A discreet bow of ribbon can also be used if desired.

Whatever method of construction is used, the same degree of good workmanship and use of design principles apply.

Bouquet handles

When finishing a handle on a bride's bouquet, the comfort of the bride is of prime concern. The bouquet may have to be held for a considerable length of time, both during and after the wedding ceremony. If the handle is uncomfortable to hold, the bride will not carry the bouquet correctly. Wires which form the handle should be kept straight and not twist around each other. During the assembly of the bouquet, consideration must be given to actual balance – each placement of flowers and foliage will affect the finished balance. If the bouquet has been made well it will be light and sit in the hand without swinging or tipping forwards or sideways.

Some handles on manufactured foam holders are padded for extra comfort. When making a handle on a wired bouquet, use a soft satin or velvet ribbon for binding. Never use a polypropylene ribbon, which is abrasive to the hand. Choose a ribbon that tones with the flowers in the bouquet. Only use a white ribbon when the colour of the flowers is predominantly white, otherwise it will be obtrusive.

Fig. 8.16   Make bow by wiring loops together. Tape this to top of handle at back of bouquet

MATERIALS

Reel of 25 mm (1″) satin ribbon – colour to tone with the flowers
Reel of gutta-percha
Glue gun or double-sided sticky tape

METHOD

1 Cut the wires and taper them neatly to form the handle (approximately 100 mm (4″) in length). The handle wires should be straight and neat; never twist them around one another.

2 Make a small bow by wiring loops together with a 0.28 mm silver wire (using the double-leg method) and tape this to the top of the handle (Fig. 8.16).

3 Tape down the length of the handle. Finish it off carefully, enclosing all the wires so that none are left exposed. Use white tape if the ribbon is a pastel colour; darker tapes will show through the ribbon.

4 Take a reel of 25 mm (1″) satin ribbon. Leaving approximately 100 mm (4″) of ribbon free, start binding firmly down the handle from above the bow (Fig. 8.17).

5 Anchor the ribbon securely to the base of the handle, using a small amount of glue or a length of double-sided sticky tape.

Fig. 8.17   Bind ribbon firmly down handle, leaving approximately 100 mm (4″) free

6 Make a neat bandage end with the ribbon at the base of the handle (*Fig. 8.18*), then wind it firmly and smoothly back up the handle. Finish binding just above the bow. The ribbon should be tightly bound so that it will not unravel when handled. Cut off the ribbon, leaving enough to tie with the other free end. Tie the ends securely above the bow and trim them to form part of the bow (*Fig. 8.19*).

Fig. 8.18   Make a neat bandage end

Fig. 8.19   Tie ends securely above bow and trim to form part of bow

Hand-tied bouquets

The simplest of all wedding bouquets, hand-tied bouquets are popular because of the versatility of styles available. Brides can choose from a simple sheaf of lilies carried over the arm to the abundance of a country bunch with a 'just picked' look. Flowers and foliage are tied together at one point. The stems are generally left free, but can be covered if desired.

It takes as much design knowledge and a greater amount of technical skill to produce a good hand-tied bouquet than for any other form of bouquet. It is a mistake to think this is a quick and easy option.

Special technical consideration must be given to hand-tied bouquets for brides and their attendants. Unlike tied bouquets made for gifts, which are designed to be placed in a vase, a bride's hand-tied bouquet will be carried for a long period of time and must look beautiful from all angles.

- The finished bouquet should be light in weight and should sit perfectly balanced in the hand.

- All stems below the binding point must be meticulously clean and free of foliage.

- Never send a bouquet out with wet stems. The water could damage an expensive gown.

- Ensure that the bouquet is tied firmly. Remember, stems that are drying out will shrink slightly. A firm tying point is therefore essential to hold the bouquet in position without damaging the flowers and their stems.

- The profile of the bouquet is as important as the top of the design. Flowers should come right down the sides of the bouquet to the tying point level, to avoid unsightly amounts of stem showing.

- Because the flowers and foliage are on longer stems, they do have a tendency to wilt more rapidly than those in conventional bouquets. This must be taken into consideration when selecting the flowers and foliage.

- Depending on the style of bouquet, the stems should be neatly spiralled or linear.

Be adventurous in choosing the flowers and plant materials. Look for materials with natural trails, such as jasmine, *Asparagus sprengeri*, bear grass and hedera, to give a cascading look. Fillers, like september, solidago, gypsophila, *Ammi majus* and *Alchemilla mollis*, will help create a light, pretty look.

Choose interesting foliage, berries, mosses, twigs and grasses, and team them with exciting colour harmonies to create a unique bouquet.

Beidermeier bouquet

The Beidermeier bouquet consists of flowers grouped tightly together in a round or pyramid shape, with all the flower heads level. Choose the shapes of the materials with care, as this style of bouquet can look visually heavy. Patterns within the design will increase the visual appeal. (*See Fig. 8.20.*)

Informal presentation bouquet

The informal presentation bouquet is a classical style which was very popular with brides in the early 1900s. It is designed to lie comfortably in the crook of the arm, with flowers and foliage cascading gracefully downwards. Flowers and foliage are used on natural stems and only support wired if absolutely necessary. The tying point is generally hidden by a discreet ribbon bow. This faced design can be symmetrical or asymmetrical in shape. The style is particularly suited to 1920s-style dresses. (*See Fig. 8.21.*)

Fig. 8.20   Beidermeier bouquet

Fig. 8.21   Informal presentation bouquet

Natural posy

The natural posy is a simple, round-shaped style, generally fashioned with small flowers which can be loosely arranged or massed. This is ideal for small bridesmaids, when a country or garden style is required. The posy is usually finished with a ring of foliage. (*See Fig. 8.22.*)

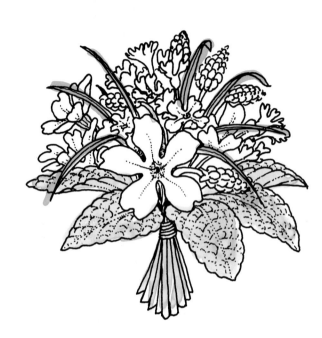

Fig. 8.22 Natural posy

Decorative posy

The decorative posy has a loose, round shape with flowers freely arranged within the outline. This is a popular choice for brides, as it can be made with a variety of materials and lovely colourings. It is also fashionable for the bride looking for a natural 'just picked' look. Flowers and foliage are used at different levels in the bouquet.

See Plate 18

There are many other styles of hand-tied bouquets. These include the following:

- Waterfall
- Textured/tufted
- Formal linear
- Vegetative

Decorative hand-tied posy

MATERIALS

10 roses
5 spray rose stems
2 sweet pea bunches
5 freesia stems
Gypsophila
5 alchemilla stems
Bear grass
Eucalyptus
Jasmine
5 large leaves (e.g. fatsia)
Rafia or tying twine
25 mm (1") satin ribbon

METHOD

1 Choose flowers without blemishes, which have been well conditioned. Prepare the flowers and foliage by removing all foliage which will be below the tying point. Clean the stems where necessary. De-thorn all the roses.

2 For easy access, place all the flowers and foliage in groups on the work bench.

3 Use a small bunch of eucalyptus to act as a support for the focal flowers (*Fig. 8.23*).

Fig. 8.23

4 The stems should neatly spiral around the central flowers. This is achieved by placing flowers and foliage from left to right at the front, and from right to left at the back of the bouquet. Keep turning the bouquet to ensure a good shape.

5 Begin by using a rose in the centre of the bouquet. Group the other roses around it, interspersing them with gypsophila and bear grass. Use eucalyptus and alchemilla between the flowers as well, to create an open effect and to achieve the circular shape.

6 Place the spray roses towards the centre of the bouquet to give bulk to the focal area. Add bear grass in small groups to give rhythm (*Fig. 8.24*).

Fig. 8.24

Remember, the stems must be spiralling neatly.

7 Keep adding gypsophila, alchemilla and eucalyptus. Use sweet peas and freesia to fill in, and gradually bring the flowers down the sides of the bouquet to the tying point.

8 Finish off the bouquet with jasmine trails and groups of bear grass placed around the edges. Neaten the base by adding four or five large leaves.

9 Firmly tie the bouquet with rafia (or similar), using enough to wrap around the stems several times before securely tying them.

10 The stems are an important part of the overall design. Cut them to a length which is easy to carry – approximately one-third of the length of the finished bouquet (*Fig. 8.25*).

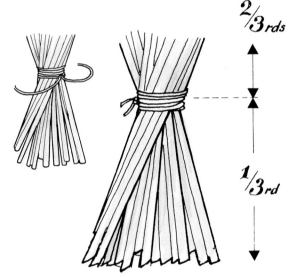

Fig. 8.25

11 Place the posy in water and keep it in a cool, dark place until just before packing.

12 Finish by drying the stems and covering the tying point with a length of ribbon and a neat bow. (Use ribbon of approximately 25 mm (1″) width.) The bow should be in proportion and never overpower the flowers.

See Plate 18

Plate 18   Decorative posy

Introduction

Most brides want some form of flower decoration for their wedding reception. This can range from one top table arrangement to a marquee full of flamboyant floral decorations. **See Plate 19.** Much will depend on the bride's budget – money will be the key factor when deciding on flowers for the wedding reception.

Sometimes the venue chosen will supply the table flowers, using their own florist. This is why it is important to discuss the church and wedding reception flowers with the bride on the initial visit. Impress upon her the need for total harmony in all the floral decor for the perfect look throughout the whole day.

Several inclusive packages can be devised for the wedding reception flowers. A simple package could contain the following:

- A garland of foliage and ribbon for the top table.
- A top table arrangement.
- Ten hand-tied posies in glass vases for the guests' tables (vases on loan).
- Two hand-tied bouquets for the bride and groom's mothers.

Once the bride has indicated her desire for reception flowers, visit the venue before making the final details. Look at the proportions of the room. Examine the room for eyesores which may need concealing, or details that should be highlighted (for example pillars, fireplace, staircase or similar). Take the opportunity to point these out to the bride. Additional sales will arise and the whole day will be uniquely co-ordinated.

Cake decoration

Decorations for wedding cakes have come a long way since the long silver vase, displaying a few freesias and fern, was placed precariously on the top tier. The style of cakes themselves has also changed dramatically, and a three-tier cake is no longer obligatory. Different styles of cake stand mean that the cakes are displayed more attractively and, generally, the cake is colour co-ordinated to the theme of the wedding. With the arrival of fondant icing, more brides have opted for iced decorations rather than fresh flowers. There is

therefore a need to sell the idea of a fresh flower decoration to the bride, emphasising the linked theme that will run throughout the wedding day.

Use the design skills at your disposal to create original styles of decoration. Flowers do not have to be limited to the top of the cake. Use bear grass or ribbons to link more than one design. Trail foliage over the edge of the cake. Garland the cake stand with old fashioned romantic flowers, or make a swag to encircle a three-tier cake. Many super designs can be created with a little thought and ingenuity.

The bride should bring in details of the style, size and colour of the cake. The decoration can then be made using this information. **Always design the cake decoration to complement the cake.** It should look an intrinsic part of it. Each cake will demand a different style and size of decoration. Proportion is the most important design principle here. A three-tier cake needs a taller design which can be made in a small vase to give extra height if necessary. This style, however, could look totally out of proportion on a single cake, where a smaller corsage-type design might be more suitable. Above all, the flower decoration should be light in weight and completely dry to avoid damage to the cake. Many methods of construction can be used and this, again, will depend on the style of the decoration. Remember, wired designs can be very time consuming to make.

MATERIALS

Foam igloo
1 lisianthus stem
3 spray rose stems
1 *Chrysanthemum parthenium* stem
2 ageratum stems
Small hedera trails and some larger leaves
September, gypsophila or similar
Nephrolepsis
Bear grass
Small piece of polythene
Wires, various gauges

METHOD

1 Soak the igloo for a few minutes, then drain off any excess water. Take a double layer of white polythene and cover the base of the igloo, securing it around the sides of the foam with tape. This will prevent water seepage.

2 Select the flowers and foliage for quality, shape and colour. Wash all the foliage carefully as it will be in close proximity to food.

3 The size of the arrangement will depend on the circumference of the cake. Before making the outline, use several hedera leaves to form a flat circle of foliage

around the base of the igloo. These will ensure a neat finish to the underside of the decoration (*Fig. 9.1*). Some stems may need a support wire.

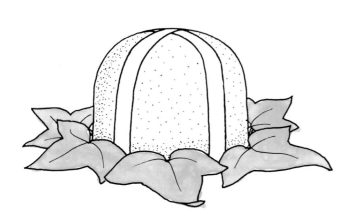

Fig. 9.1 Use hedera leaves to form flat circle of foliage around base of igloo

Fig. 9.2 Establish height and width of arrangement

4 Place a tall piece of september, plus a few strands of bear grass, in the centre of the igloo. This will determine the height of the arrangement. Use hedera trails, september and small nephrolepsis fronds in groups around the base of the igloo. Position them on top of the larger leaves already in place. This will form the outline and establish the height and width of the arrangement (*Fig. 9.2*).

5 Use two of the open spray roses on either side of the design, grouping them with the smallest at the top and the larger roses in the central positions. Take two hedera leaves and place them around the focal flowers for added emphasis (*Fig. 9.3*).

6 Group the other spray roses, september and *Chrysanthemum parthenium* through the design, recessing some low into the arrangement.

7 Choose small, open lisianthus and group them at the sides of the design.

8 Fill in where necessary, taking care not to spoil the design by overcrowding. Ensure that all the foam is covered. *Chrysanthemum parthenium* is especially good for recessing in small groups at varying levels. Remember that the arrangement will be seen from all sides.

Fig. 9.3 Placement of roses

9 The decoration can then be finished in several ways. For example, long strands of bear grass can be placed around the design, below the central flowers, to drape gracefully over the sides of the cake. One or two tiny flowers can then be glued carefully to this. Alternatively, two small gold rings, or ribbons plaited or tied with lovers knots, can be added. Whichever method is used, meticulous attention to detail must be applied for a professional finish.

10 Spray the decoration lightly with water and place it in a cool, dark room, covered with polythene, until needed.

See Plate 20

Knife decoration

To complement the cake arrangement, a small decoration can be made to attach to the cake knife. Make a small bow from a luxury satin ribbon, in a colour to match the cake and flowers. Construct a simple nosegay or corsage using the same varieties as those in the cake arrangement. Tie these into the centre of the ribbon bow with a long narrow ribbon. These streamers of ribbon will tie around the handle to secure the decoration to the knife.

See Plate 20

Gifts

The bride may wish to give gifts at the reception to relatives or anyone who has helped with her wedding plans. She will probably discuss this, or you can suggest it when she orders her wedding bouquets.

A floral gift has immediate impact on the recipient and is the ideal present to give at a wedding reception. There is a whole host of designs and the choice should never be restricted to gift-wrapped flowers in cellophane. Remember, it can be a very hot atmosphere at a wedding reception and the recipient will want to take the flowers home in perfect condition. Consideration must therefore be given to the lasting qualities of the gift. A basket of flowers is most suitable – it is easy to carry and allows the flowers and foliage to drink from the water-retaining foam during the reception. A hand-tied bouquet also makes a lovely gift. If water is added to the cellophane base, this must be removed before presentation. **Never give a presentation bouquet with water in the base.** Water seepage can occur if the bouquet is not held upright and this could cause damage to an expensive gown.

Whatever style of floral gift chosen, try to link the choice of colour and flowers to the overall wedding theme.

Plate 19   Wedding reception flowers

Plate 20   Cake and knife decorations

AFTERCARE

Introduction

Wedding bouquets are made with great care and expertise, and many hours are allocated to their concept and assembly. The caring does not stop until the bride walks down the aisle with her beautiful bouquet.

Once the bouquets have been completed, they should be sprayed lightly with water, completely enclosed in polythene, and packed in a cool room or similar to rest until the final packaging begins.

Any hand-tied bouquets can be placed in water, adding the ribbon trimmings just before placing them in the wedding box.

Before the bouquets are packed for delivery, all the wedding flowers should be scrutinised. Look for any flowers which have faded, replace any suspect foliage, finish off wired bouquets by ribboning the handles and, generally, make any last minute adjustments. A few minutes checking the order and studying the bouquets now could correct an oversight.

Allocate plenty of time for packing the order and delivering it to the bride's home. Aim to have the bouquets at the bride's home at least one and a half hours before the wedding. Tell the bride the approximate delivery time in advance. Brides become very agitated if they think the flowers are late.

Bridal bouquets need special handling and care while in transit. Ensure the driver knows how to handle the bouquets and to present them to the bride.

Presentation and packaging

One of the highlights of a wedding morning is the arrival of the flowers. Everyone crowds eagerly around the bride for the first viewing of the bouquets. The bride's sense of anticipation should be followed by instant expressions of delight as the boxes are carefully unwrapped and the bouquets are gently lifted out. Here is a happy moment that the bride and her entourage will always remember – the name of your florist shop will be remembered with it.

The presentation and packaging of the bouquets is vitally important to give immediate appeal. The method of packaging will depend on the quantity of bouquets and their style. A bride's bouquet looks impressive if laid on top of a flower box lid then wrapped with a cellophane cover. Hand-tied bouquets are best packed inside a box. Whichever method is chosen, the packaging should protect the flowers while in transit and enhance their appearance.

The presentation box with the wedding bouquet in can be trimmed, if desired, with special wedding ribbons or a sprig of white heather. Often, the bride will press one or two flowers from her wedding bouquet as a keepsake. A small gift of these flowers with a card can be added to the box as a unique and personal present.

Always send care instructions with the bouquets (*Fig. 10.1*). These can be printed for a professional appearance but, alternatively, a neat handwritten note reflects the personal service you give.

Dear
Your wedding bouquets have been designed with great care for your special day. Excessive handling will damage the delicate blooms. Please keep your bouquets in the box until just before the ceremony. Place the box in a dark cool place on arrival, away from direct sunlight and heat. If your bouquets are in the hand-tied fashion with stems left free, you can place the flowers in water at the reception.

Have a lovely day

Fig. 10.1   Care instructions

The instructions should advise how to handle the flowers, where to place them until the ceremony, and give any other information of use to the bride. The bride will also need advice on how to carry the bouquet. This can be done in the shop, at the consultation, when the bride can practise with an artificial bouquet, or it can be added to the care instructions.

Packaging a bouquet

MATERIALS

Flower box (size big enough to lie the bouquet
    on comfortably)
6 plant sticks (approximately 300 mm (12"))
Shop wrapping paper
Cellofilm
Glue
Clear adhesive tape

METHOD

1 Use a clean, dry, flower box – preferably with no
   printing on it. Make sure the bouquet will fit on top of
   the box comfortably.

2 Wrap the whole box and lid together, using your shop's
   wrapping paper. When wrapped, the box should look
   neat and professional.

3 Make an insertion at each corner of the box and glue
   four plant sticks securely into place. Also glue two plant
   sticks into the centre of the box to form a cage for the
   cellofilm (*Fig. 10.2*). For a very neat finish, these can be
   taped with a white tape.

4 Place the bouquet in a central position on top of the lid.
   Make an insertion in the box so that the handle of the
   bouquet will slot through it – the bouquet should then
   rest gently on the lid. If necessary, tissue paper can be
   used beneath the bouquet for extra support.

5 Spray the bouquet well.

6 Cover the top of the box with cellofilm, using the plant
   sticks to create a cage for the cellofilm to rest on. This
   will prevent the packaging from damaging the flowers,
   and will also give a very neat, square top to the cellofilm
   wrapping.

7 Attach delivery and care instructions to the side of the
   box.

See Plate 21

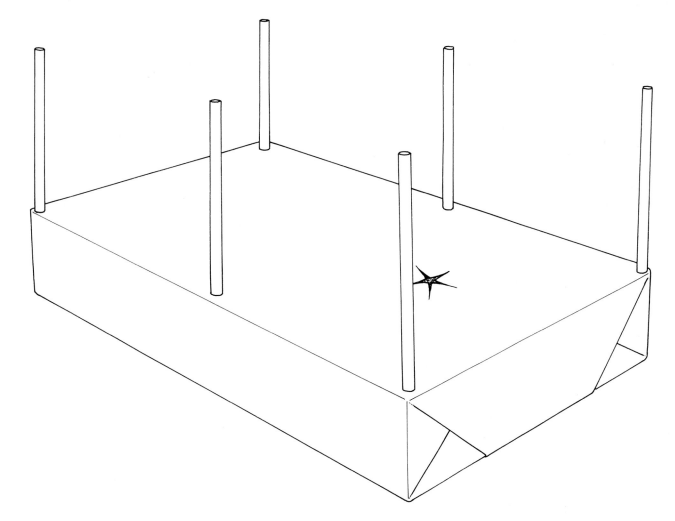

Fig. 10.2

AFTERCARE

10

Plate 21   An attractively packaged bouquet